Time Alone with God

Lee Veasman Rose

Remember
The Lord covered all sin at the cross— great
or small— including typos and proofing
flaws.
            In Christ's love
                    Lee Rose

Published by Lee Veasman Rose

Copyright © 2017 Lee Veasman Rose

ISBN-13: 978-1979764070
ISBN-10: 1979764077

Dedication

To my parents, Husted and Fannie Mae Veasman, whose lives of faith, courage, and vision have been my inspiration.

To my husband, Paul L. Rose who was my loving life partner for 52 years.

For my children, Kelly Rose Hall and Glen Husted Rose and their families whom I love dearly.

Acknowledgements

Betty Handlin—whose friendship developed over the years as both of us sat in front of the computer screen with our cups of coffee in hand-- pushed, pulled, and dragged me kicking and screaming into the world of technology. Without her encouragement, patience, and knowledge as she introduced me to new programs and gadgets, I might still be using a slate and handwritten materials. Thank you, Betty, but thanks is not enough.

Paul Anderson helped me through all the technical aspects of this venture. I was told how competent he was in this area of expertise and how patient he was with others' incompetence; both comments were understatements. I could not have finished compiling this manuscript without him. Without his advice and invaluable assistance, this book would still be in bits and pieces. It was he who brought about the completion of it all and I am truly grateful to him.

Dr. Rick Webb was just the person I needed to proof the content and find my errors. Isn't that the way it works? I can see the speck in your eye, but I can't see the beam in my own. Thank you for your spiritual guidance. Your efforts continue to be appreciated.

Members of my Gleaners Life Group gave me encouragement as they read small portions of my whining and nagging that I euphemistically call "conversations with the Lord." Their love and acceptance of me as I grieved "the downsizing of my life" has meant more than they will ever know. I don't want to imagine what the transition would have been like without them.

God provided caring people in Longview; and they welcomed and supported me as I started this stage of my life. The third day I was in Longview, my daughter, Kelly Hall, took me to Heartisans and introduced me to Julee Rachels. I knew I had found my niche to start over. Living at Buckner has been a safe, spiritual oasis—an atmosphere of neighborly, family living. I hesitate to mention others by name because I am sure I would overlook someone who has been equally meaningful to me. Along the way, there have been angels of all descriptions, sizes, and shapes and I am grateful for each one.

Contents

Fasting or Feasting

Fasting or Feasting

Teach me to realize the brevity of life, so that I may grow in wisdom and please you. (Psalm 90:12).

- *First:* I will be quiet as I come before you, Lord. I will sit down and shut up.
- *Second:* I will pray asking for an open mind and to be cleansed.
- *Third:* I will read the scripture slowly and let you speak to me. I will think about your message for me.
- *Fourth:* I will meditate and think about it again.
- *Fifth:* I will write down what I learned so I'll be more likely to remember it.
- *Sixth:* And, I will pray again, asking to see your message because it is written to me and for me. I will talk to you about everything.

40 Days

40 days of rain changed Noah's life; 40 days on Mt. Sinai changed Moses; 40 days in the Promised Land changed the spies; Goliath's 40-day challenge changed David; Elijah received 40 days of Strength from a single meal; Nineveh was transformed in 40 days and Jesus was empowered by 40 days in the alone wilderness with the Father. Lord, during the next 40 days, I want to feast on your Word and grow through a special time with you—my TAG—my Time Alone with God!.

Lord, I write for my sake and as a record of your Presence with me. Each TAG is a treasure. If any of them can be of benefit to someone else or used to your glory, praise your name. If not, they still have been my treasure. They are not to be seen as "an act of righteousness before others." (Matthew 6:1).

Each TAG is just a reminder of conversation with you, Lord, and sharing is standing on your Word that where there are two or more gathered in your name you will be with us.

— *Day 1* —

Lord, you are a great and awesome God who keeps your promises and who is so loving and kind to those who love and obey you. Hear my prayer. Listen to me, Lord. We—I, my family, and this nation—have sinned against you and disobeyed your commandments. May we turn to you, looking for forgiveness and guidance. (Nehemiah 1:4—10).

You tell me to bring my requests to you. (Philippians 4:6). I am bringing my concerns to you now—and knowing me, I'll bring the same ones to you again tomorrow and then again the next day. You know I am a professional nag!

Thank you for the peace you give me when I do bring my concerns to you and trust you with the outcomes. (Isaiah 26:3). Lessons of trust come wrapped in difficulties—but I want to learn them regardless of the circumstances.

This a.m. I thank you for all the blessings you have already provided and ask for a continued awareness of your strength, power, presence, and love.

Joshua 24:15 is my mantra. Love, honor, thanksgiving belong to you. Let your Word continue to "be a lamp to my feet and a light for my path." (Psalm 119:105).

— *Day 2* —

Lord, thank you for allowing me to come to you this a.m., finding peace with you. I want to follow your Word. (Philippians 4:8). I will "fix my thoughts on what is true, good, and right. I will think about things that are pure and lovely and dwell on the fine, good things in others. I will ponder on all that I can praise you for and all that I can be glad about."

Lord, when there is a surprise illness, it is only a surprise to me. I can trust that it is not a surprise to you. May I "take every thought captive" and bring my fears and concerns to you. (2 Corinthians 10:5). I will focus on the truth that is in front of me: God is faithful, good, loving, and sovereign; and you and the Father are one. In you, there is peace.

I will praise you and God, the Father, for a well-timed doctor's appointment and the simple gift of another day. Knowing that the two of you are not surprised by this situation is a special gift.

The faith road isn't easy, but I am asked to trust and be obedient. When I am fearful, I am questioning your character and that of the Father. Forgive me. He is perfect and his timing is perfect.

In this season of uncertainty, I can trust his faithfulness—not just for eternity but also for tomorrow and right now.

— *Day 3* —

Lord, I am yours. Today, may I walk closely with you each moment, listening for your voice, enjoying your companionship, holding tightly to your hand. (John 10:4).

Lord, today "my pleas are for those you have given me." (John 17:9b). Forgive me for misappropriating your Word, but we so desperately need you in our lives individually and in our relationships with each other. And your Word says it so perfectly.

May we be filled with your joy. (John 17:13b). Lord, I am not asking you to take them out of the world, but keep them and me safe from Satan's power. (John 17:15). May each of us be ready to serve you. May we be unified in you so that others will know we are yours and then they too will believe in you. All this to say that Joshua 24:15 is my decision again this morning.

Lord, I ask for a greater awareness of your omnipresence; and I am not asking that just for the next 40 days, but for my lifetime, starting today. I want to know you, Lord, more deeply; I am asking you to enter the private areas of my mind and heart.

Thank you for the assurance that you know me and want a relationship with me. (Psalm 139:1-3). That's too wonderful for me to understand. That's intimate, unconditional, unfathomable love!

May I abide in you today and be ready to serve you.

I love you, Lord.

— *Day 4* —

I am thanking you for being here for this TAG, Lord. That's my first priority—before I begin the "help me, give me" prayers. I love you, Lord. You are so patient with me and all my weaknesses and quirks.

Today, may I see the opportunities you provide for me to share your love and to praise who you are, my Lord and Savior. I lift up each of my family and my brothers and sisters in Christ. May we leave footprints that will lead others to you.

May I sow peace where there is discord. It is good and pleasant when we live together in harmony. (Psalm 133:1). Help me love—in and through you—those with whom I disagree. Unless the topic is one that you disagree with, may I set aside the notion that my way is the only way. May I listen as you would listen—respectfully—and may we accept one another in love.

You are honored when I humbly love those who are different—as well as those who have difficulty remembering—you created us all. I want my love to mirror yours. May I have your grace to consider other viewpoints and live out the idea that loving others is more important than being right—that is, unless you say, "There is no other way."

I love you, Lord, and am committed to Joshua 24:15. I love, honor, and praise you today.

— Day 5 —

Thank you over and over—again and again—for being in the "transformation business." You work miracles today just as you did that day in Cana when you turned water into wine. (John 2:1-11).

Thank you for your sovereignty over all things. You can fit everything into a pattern for my good, (Romans 8:28), but only to the extent that I trust you. Though many incidents and circumstances seem random, you are still in charge. Every circumstance can teach me, so help me see them as they are—teachers—and give thanks. Open my mind to the possibility of benefits that could come from this situation. Help me remember all the details of Joseph being taken in slavery to Egypt; you used that situation to save your people. (Genesis 50:20).

Knowing these things, why do I not bring everything to you? You may not remove my problem; it may be a blessing in disguise. Your wisdom is sufficient to use all things to your glory. Help me learn to pray asking for your wisdom and your perspective—seeing "IT" with your eyes.

Lord, I renew my Joshua 24:15 decision again today. Bind Satan from my house for your glory. My love, praise, and thanks belong to you.

— *Day 6* —

Lord, I just want to continue on the path with you today—enjoying your presence, holding your hand, listening for your voice, growing closer to you, and knowing you better.

I know God, the Father, saved me completely because I came to him through you and you live to intercede for me. (Hebrews 7:25). You and the Father are unified with the Holy Spirit who lives in me. On that, I can come to you in confidence, knowing I will receive mercy and find grace to glorify you even in a time of need. (Hebrews 4:16).

When I come to you with my requests, may my motives be to glorify you. May the Holy Spirit guide my thoughts. Help me be aware of you at all times. Satan disguises himself in worry, envy, bitterness, jealousy, guilt, fear, anxiety, insecurity, and on and on. May I be so snuggly wrapped in your love that none of this can touch me. Lord, you know that—without **you**—I am susceptible to all these things, in addition to pride. Hold me close.

Joshua 24:15 is my decision. May I use your name and your power to bind Satan from me and my house that you may be glorified. Lord, I trust you and ask you to strengthen the trust I have.

Love, honor, praise and thanksgiving are yours.

— *Day 7* —

Lord, these are scattered, disjointed thoughts I bring to you this a.m.; but the first thing I bring is a sincere thank you for your saving grace and your continual presence. Thank you for your strength and help that is available to get me through this day. I have a choice to be dreary and downcast as I go it alone or to walk joyously in dependence on you. That is my choice each day; it's the difficulties that highlight the decision-making process. (James 1:2-3). "You are my help and I will rejoice as I cling to you. (Psalm 63:7-8).

Lord, I am asking for a fresh faith today—one that is based on your Word. I am repenting so my sins and shame can be wiped out and so I can receive "the seasons of refreshing that are there for me in your presence." Lord, I never want to twist your Word just to suit me. I simply write to remind me of the foundation of my thought. (Acts 3:19-20). And you are the God of fresh starts.

Lord, you are also a "Because-I-said-so" God. If you said it, it is so—it is true. I want to respond to you joyfully because I know there is great benefit in believing Matthew 21:22: Belief + Prayer= Receiving. May I learn GPT and let my faith grow.

My commitment to serve you remains. (Joshua 24:15).

Love, praise, honor, thanksgiving all belong to you.

— *Another thought, Lord, on Day 7* —

"Because I said so…"

The thief on the cross prayed. "Jesus, remember me when you come into your kingdom." (Luke 23:42).

By this time, everyone in the area knew of the miracles you had done and could do.

Although the thief's pain would have been excruciating—because he too had the nails driven into his hands—he didn't ask for pain relief. He didn't even ask for you to save him from death.

He said, "Jesus, remember me" because he knew his deepest need was salvation from his sin. He believed in you, Lord. You replied to that criminal hanging there on the cross with you, "I assure you, today, you will be with me in paradise." (Luke 23:43b).

Lord, your Word tells me (Acts 16:31) "Believe in the Lord Jesus, and you will be saved." It is by grace I have been saved, through faith—and that grace is not from me—it is a gift from you. I couldn't work to earn it so I can't boast about it. (Ephesians 2:8-9).

The thief was saved that day and so am I—because you said so!

— *Day 8* —

Thank you, Lord, for this TAG! This time is not for anyone else, it's my time with you—just my time with the Creator of the universe, the King of kings, Jesus who hung on the cross for me, and Jesus the Resurrected Savior!

Lord, so often I look back at last week—or sections of my life—and wish for a "do over." There's the memory of the mess I made: errors in judgment, things left undone, unkind words spoken, missed opportunities, poor example set for others. What a load to carry!

Thank you for the relief I find when I come to you asking forgiveness for the mess I've made of things—life in general. You took the anger, defeat, destruction, and all the other garbage. I don't have to carry that any more.

As soon as I asked for your forgiveness of "the past," I could come to you asking for your wisdom and guidance for the days ahead. That was a fresh start. You are the God of fresh starts. And I can have a fresh start anytime I ask for it.

Here with you I find peace, healing, hope. But, Lord, I don't want to limit you by my unbelief or by thinking "I know" all that you can do. (Ephesians 3:20). In you, all things are possible. You are infinite.

Today, my decision is Joshua 24:15, and I do ask for your power to bind Satan from me and my house.

— *Day 9* —

Lord, yes, again this a.m. I thank you for allowing me to come to you. The world spins faster and faster—so it seems. Here with you I can find calm and be energized as you fill me with your love, joy, and peace. (Galatians 5:22). Here, as I depend on you, I can allow your power to replace my weaknesses.

As a believer, I am "to walk by faith, not by sight." (2 Corinthians 5:7). I wonder how many miracles I have missed because of my lack of faith? How many times I have questioned you instead of accepting you at your Word? If I had been the lame man at the pool, (John 5:1-8), would I have gotten up and walked as soon as you said "Get up!"? Lord, I want my faith to grow so that I take the step as soon as you tell me to. I want my life to glorify you every day.

As I look at your Word, I see you told the older generation to teach the younger. In Deuteronomy 4:14, I see I am to teach others and not forget what you have shown me and taught me. Forgive me where I have failed in the past to do that. Today, Lord, show me how to make a generational connection with my family and others that will bring harmony and peace—and draw them closer to you.

I am yours. Turn my weakness to strength and my foolishness to heavenly wisdom. You have my permission to interrupt my plans and use me.

I am repeating myself once again: My Joshua 24:15 commitment remains and is my prayer. The power of your name can bind Satan from me and my family; thank you for letting me use it. May the glory be yours.

— *Day 10* —

Lord, I am yours for all time and even eternally. This morning I come to experience you, to be exposed to your amazing greatness. I want my eyes and ears opened to all of you.

Your faithfulness is astounding! You have kept every promise for thousands of generations (Deuteronomy 7:9) and you keep them today. You aren't slow; you are just patiently waiting for our repentance. (2 Peter 3:9). Show me how to be more available to you. You use such "extraordinary measures" to show your love to me—such an ordinary person.

Knowing my future in you is secure, I want to live in response to you, (Psalm 37:23-24), to be a reflection of you. You have forgiven me; help me forgive others—each one. (Luke 6:37-38). Help me treat each of your children with the same kindness and generosity you have given me. It is here that I really need your help, Lord. Expand that to: I really need your help all the time, wherever I am. Without your guidance and your powerful right hand holding me, I fail.

Today help me be open to all you can do and are doing. Don't let my limited mind tell you what to do—you can do more for me than I can ask for or even imagine. (Ephesians 3:20).

Lord, I am yours and I will serve you all the days of my life. In your right hand, I am safe from Satan's schemes and taunts.

My love, honor, and praise go to you.

— *Day 11* —

Lord, this morning give me an open mind ready to hear you deep within my heart. I want an active, authentic prayer life that keeps me in constant communication with you.

I cannot be your disciple if I don't pick up my cross and follow you. (Luke 14:27). I want to know specifically how to do that daily. I want to hear your voice.

I am to walk by faith and not by sight (2 Corinthians 5:7) and I want to keep in step with your Spirit. (Galatians 5:25). Show me what you can do for me. Is it my lack of faith that keeps you from performing obvious miracles as you did "back then"? Do I live my life too safely, limiting you? Do I keep the Spirit from working in me? Forgive me, Lord. Grow me, Lord.

I am weak, but you know that. You gave me your Spirit so I could live beyond my natural ability and strength. The issue is not your strength, but my failure to utilize your strength and power—which is limitless.

Today I want to walk close to you, picking up my cross, following you, accomplishing your purposes for my life. I want to take the next "right" step.

When I am defeated and afraid, Lord, please pour your healing grace into every crack of my life, pick me up, and give me a fresh start. (Psalm 147:3). Now, I again pray Joshua 24:15.

You deserve all my love, honor, praise and more.

— *Day 12* —

Lord, thank you for letting me come to you and just sit, waiting—waiting hopefully to dine with you—waiting at your table's smorgasbord of kindness, patience, wisdom, instruction, grace, forgiveness, peace, strength, and courage. Oh! the taste of it. (Psalm 34:8).

You have prepared and continue to provide everything I need to survive—abundantly. You provided for Elijah when you sent the raven to feed him and when the widow made bread for him that lasted and lasted. Lord, you have always been in the miracle business and are even today. Thank you for the miracle of being able to know you, to be in your presence, to hear your whispers.

Lord, you told Elijah that part of his loneliness was based on ignorance. It looks like Elijah and I have something—a lot—in common. I struggle with feeling alone and being fearful even after you have comforted me and reassured me of your constant love and care.

You have things for me to do even in the midst of my fear and failures; and you always have more resources than I am aware of. Thank you, Lord. You know I would like to see one of your spectacular and unusual miracles, but I am thankful that you still—often—speak through the gentle and obvious circumstances around me. May I focus on deepening my relationship with you so I can recognize you are at work in me.

Joshua 24:15 is my decision today and I love and praise you.

Afterthought: I am to love others as they are at this very moment; not as I would like for them to be.

— *Day 13* —

Lord, thank you for being here with me now (4:00 a.m.) and for your Word. All your Word is perfect and some of it is so precious to me that I go back to familiar parts over and over. You tell me you have examined me and know all about me. (Psalm 139:1).

You know my every thought—my standing or sitting (2). You have a plan for me and will guide me (3)—if I will let you. You know where I am. You know what I am going to say before I say it. (4) You go before me. (5). Why am I afraid? You will be there in any situation waiting for me to show up. You are behind me. (5). Nothing or no one can sneak up/overtake me without your permission. You bless me. Yes, thank you for being here with me this morning.

You know me personally and intimately. You know me intricately because you formed me. As a Friend, you know what makes me happy or sad. As a Friend, you want me to bring both my victories and failures to you. The WOW is: I am friends with the Almighty God who has written me a love letter and will give me deeper insight into his desires for me. He will show me his way for me.

I want to learn to trust you 100% with every aspect of my life.

Lord, I want to learn acceptance; teach me. The devil is out there; bind him from me and my family, Lord. You have my love, honor, praise and thanksgiving.

Referencing Daniel 9:3

Daniel struck deep within me this morning when he said, "So I turned my attention to the Lord, God, to seek him by prayer and petitions, with fasting, sackcloth, and ashes."

Many things can hold me in captivity—the list is endless. Daniel knew the 70-year captivity was ending and his role would change. He wanted guidance in his new role so he came to you, Lord, confessing his sin.

Lord, you know I was not prepared for the "change of roles" in my life when my children left the nest and began creating lives of their own. Then, the change when grandchildren began creating their own lives. Then, the change when I became an old widow.

I'm afraid I didn't plant the spiritual roots you would have liked in the lives of my children when they were at a tender age and in my care. I would like a "do over." Since a "do over" isn't possible, I am asking your forgiveness.

Today, I turn my attention to you, seeking you in prayer and petitions, with fasting. My parental role has changed; I must restrain myself. Lord, keep my mouth shut until you give me the words. Saying too much, meddling, sounding preachy can destroy my relationships with them. When I have a concern, let me bring it to you, leave it there until you have in it in GPT and seasoned it with love.

Today may my life's example serve as an influence. Teach me when to speak and when to be still. Let me be the example you want for others when a silent sermon is what they need the most. Help me learn to pray specifically for "their awakening" and that I be obedient to you in my own life.

Continued on page 18...

...Continued from page 17

Lord, sometimes the concerns are so strong and the pain so intense, I can hardly handle it. An old friend, Martha Ann, who loved you dearly, once told me "***Close your eyes***, Lee. You are in charge of everyone and everything ***you can see*** at this moment. Now pray!" Another one said, "Pray for your kids and grandkids with a 'whatever-it-takes' attitude before the Lord. Ask God to do whatever it takes to draw them into his will—***not into your will***, Lee."

I want to do that, but sometimes the words almost won't come out of my mouth. Then, I have prayed that with fear because I know some of your ways seem harsh—but I also know your ways are higher than mine. (Isaiah 55:9-11).

You didn't give me children and grandchildren to make me look good. You gave them to me for your purposes, so they might be in a relationship with you and bring you glory.

I bring my parental failures to you asking forgiveness and leaving them with you. Now, I turn my attention to you in prayer for me and each of my adult family. Lord, you have my permission to interfere in our lives so we may be drawn into a closer relationship with you and closer to each other. May each of us humble ourselves at your feet.

Remind me to love others as they are at this moment; not as I want them to be. I love and praise you, Lord.

— *Day 14* —

Lord, thank you for the Joy you bring so abundantly. Here in the quiet, your blessing can flow to me more freely. Here you are freer to transform me (Romans 12:2) to your likeness. Here I can realize how wide, long, deep, and wide your love is (Ephesians 3:17-19) and that I am wrapped in it. It almost seems too good to be true; however, I will just "Be still and know you are God—and your love is true."

Thank you that the moment I don't know how to pray, your Spirit is right alongside me, helping me. When deep within me, my soul cries out of an intense need, fear, or even gratitude—but no words come— you hear me. You are there, praying for me, understanding and making words out of my sighs and my longings. I have confidence that because I love you, you are working something good for me. (Romans 8:26-28).

Lord, now that I am old and gray, I know you won't forsake me. (Psalm 71:18). I have seen your faithfulness throughout the years and you are never changing—immutable! I ask you to give me time to tell this new generation—and their children—about your love, your faithfulness, and all that you do for us.

Today, I am again committing to your service (Joshua 24:15) and I'm using the power of your name to bind Satan from me and my house.

My love, honor, praise, and thanksgiving belong to you.

— *Day 15* —

Lord, I come this a.m. listening for your voice and I hear you singing your love song to me. (Zephaniah 3:17). You continue day after day telling me, showing me how much you love me. (John 3:16). Thank you for your Word. Open my heart as I seek you so I can know you more deeply.

I know you will pour out your blessings if I will just be still and listen, waiting expectantly. (Matthew 7:7).

Not only do I want to know you more, Lord, I also want to be more like you. You were on the cross and you asked the Father to "Forgive them" and that includes me. Now your instruction to me is "Be gentle and ready to forgive, never hold grudges." (Colossians 3: 12-13). I am to practice tenderhearted mercy and kindness. Thank you for telling me to "practice" because that is not my nature; that's why I am asking for transformation. (Romans 12:2).

You tell me to "be kind and compassionate to one another, forgiving... as God forgave me in you." (Ephesians 4:32). And I really need to "practice forgiveness." I have no right to withhold forgiveness when I so desperately need your and God's forgiveness. Help me offer forgiveness to others without reservation, because I want to be a reflection of you.

Lord, I am committed to serving you. (Joshua 24:15). I know I am wrapped in your robe of righteousness, but there is still much transforming to be done in me.

I love you and ask you to bind Satan from me and my house.

— *Day 16* —

Lord, thank you for being here with me again this morning. The early morning hours are my best time with you and your Word. I bring my pen and journal to keep me focused, and they provide a way to document your faithfulness to me. I also think it helps me remember to take our time together further—throughout the day. Maybe that's your gentle whispers I hear because I know you are always with me. (Joshua 1:5, 9).

Lord, you only have to "say the word" and everything will be as it should be. You healed the centurion's son with just a word. (Matthew 8:8). You created the heavens and the earth with just a word. (Genesis 1:3). You haven't changed; you still have that same power. Let my trust be as strong as the centurion's!

Your Word tells me to ask. (Matthew 7:7-8). Lord, as we walk together today, let me hear your gentle whispers reminding me to bring every care to you. Then, knowing you only give good gifts (Matthew 7:9), I will watch, wait, listen expectantly for you to provide what is best for me. Whatever your answer, it will be better than anything I could hope for or imagine. (Ephesians 3:20).

Thank you that I am weak and limited. That simply brings me to your strength. You are my strength!

Joshua 24:15 is my commitment and I am a name dropper today: your name against Satan and that's no test! You are victorious.

I love, praise, and give you thanks!

— *Day 17* —

Lord, your Word is right and true, and I thank you for it. Each day I come to you asking you to care for, lead, guide, protect "me and mine." Thank you for that privilege. Your Word (1 Timothy 2:1-2) tells me to pray for all people, intercede for them and give thanks. Lord, you don't stop there; you specifically tell me to pray for those in authority.

Lord, I am asking that all our leaders (nation, state, city, church, family) have their hearts turned to you. May their lives be marked with godliness and honesty.

You tell me not to worry about anything—just give thanks for things as they are now and bring my concerns to you. (Philippians 4:6). You are sovereign, in control of all things—so I can rest in peace. Your peace replaces my panic. (4:7).

Help me dwell on whatever is true, honorable, just, pure, lovely, commendable! Help me put into practice what you have already taught me. (4:8). In you, there is peace! You know all about me, (Psalm 139:1-4) and you know how much I need you as I "practice and fail" at this admonition! It's here I say a great big "Thank you" for never leaving me (Joshua 1:5, 9) and for your grace and mercy.

Lord, thank you that I can say "I am a child of the King." Yes, that calls for more responsibility, but it gives me so many special privileges. My Daddy loves me and forgives me.

Joshua 24:15. Do I need to say more than I love, praise, honor, and give thanks?

— *Day 18* —

Lord, I am not an orphan; I have a heavenly Father who is a perfect Parent—who is all wise, all seeing and does everything in my life for my benefit so that I can share in his holiness. (Hebrews 12:10). I am thankful for that.

Thank you for loving me enough to correct me, train me, even punish me so that I am drawn close to you. Your discipline isn't pleasant, but it is evidence of your deep love for me. Help me see quickly what I am to learn from this situation.

"Have a good day!" Already I have said that to the lady at the "coffee pot". What is a "good day"? Help me redefine what is a good day. You are calling me to something different, unique, fulfilling, eternal, bigger, and Good! Help me make choices that allow you to be fully in charge—that would be a good day.

Instead of my thinking about my schedule, clothes, hair, food—and, of course, my coffee—and how other people treat me, help me think about others as you do. Help me see others as you see them. They may be someone who loves you or they may be lost, without hope because they don't know you. You love us all!

May my "Good Day" be one where I see others as you see them—each one precious to you! Help me treat them that way—each one precious to you!

Joshua 24:15. Bind Satan from me and my house so that you are glorified.

My love, praise, thanks go to you.

— *Day 19* —

Lord, I am so glad I can come to you any time of day—or night. I missed my morning TAG and I can tell it! You are the Vine and I am a branch. (John 15:5). Apart from you I can do nothing.

I have not been apart from you today. I have been to both early and late life group studies and church in between. Then this afternoon I went to church again, but I haven't had my early morning TAG.

Peter and John were suddenly filled with your courage and confidence—so much so that others could tell they had been with you. (Acts 4:13). I too want to live so close to you that others can see the difference in me. Lord, I need to start early in the day, seeking you and your righteousness if I want to get the full impact of your presence. (Matthew 6:33).

My salvation was complete the moment I believed in you as the Son of God, Savior of the world, my Savior—the Messiah, but I am still a work in process. Lord, continue this transformation until I become like you. (Romans 12:2).

May there be nothing more important to me than you! My decision is to serve you. (Joshua 24:15). Draw my house close to you and bind Satan from us.

You have my love, praise, honor, and thanks.

— *Day 20* —

Lord, this morning I just want to bring you "thank you, thank you, and thank you." My thanks can never be enough for all you have done for me, but hopefully your spirit will work freely within me to stir more thankfulness until I am overflowing with gratitude. Through your power and outpouring of love, may I give hope and encouragement to others. (2 Corinthians 5:5).

Lord, you know my farm background and know I get a clear picture when David talks about "bearing delicious fruit each season without fail" (Psalm 1:3) and when Paul says "keep on, don't give up, and we will reap at the proper time." (Galatians 6:9).

Oh, Lord, it takes faith to work the land and plant the seed and wait! Waiting when there is too much rain and a need to replant—waiting when there is no rain. Paul reminds me "not to get tired of doing good." Help me master the art of waiting—waiting in you—waiting for you.

But, I do get the picture in the planting and reaping analogy—we do reap what we sow. (Galatians 6:7). Help me never grow tired of sowing the seeds of love, joy, peace, patience, kindness, goodness, faithfulness, gentleness, and self-control—that your spirit planted in me. (Galatians 6:22). May I cultivate those seeds—never tiring and waiting expectantly. The harvest will come.

This a.m. I reaffirm my Joshua 24:15 decision with love and praise.

— *Day 21* —

Lord, thanks for being here when I finally showed up for my TAG. A day without this quiet time is really no day at all! When I come to this time seeking your presence in prayer, quietly reading your Word, you give me new purpose and meaning regardless of my age or my stage—widowhood.

Lord, grow my faith and change my perspective so much that I find the courage to do things that I cannot do on my own power. As I lean on you, empower me, Lord. May I live in such a way that others will see my life as grounded in you.

Your Word is true; you are my strength, my song, my salvation. (Isaiah 12:2-3) I will trust you, will not be afraid, and will live joyously free in you. There is joy just being in your presence. (Psalm 21:6).

Your power is unlimited; you created the universe with just a word; you healed the centurion's son with just a word; help me concentrate on that and come to you, bringing my neediness. Continue to show me areas of weakness so I can confess them to you and, with your power, overcome them. Is it my lack of faith in your power or my greediness and ego that won't allow you to work your miracles in me?

Lord, I say "the same power that raised you from the dead is the same power that lives in me today." Help me live and walk in faith, surrendered to you.

Pitiful as I am, I am committed to serving you. Bind Satan from me in all of his disguises. I love, praise, and give you thanks.

— *Day 22* —

Lord, as I walk with you today, I will rejoice and be thankful for each step. (Philippians 4:4). I will trust you and allow your peace to flow into me as you lift me up. (Psalm 9:10). Oh, what a great God you are! May I never stop singing your praises; you are my Rock, my Refuge, and my Salvation.

May today's walk with you take me on this journey learning to love unconditionally as you have loved me. As I seek your will, help me listen and hear your guidance.

Lord, thank you for your blessing as you are rewriting the mistakes I made as a young wife and mother. (Titus 2:4-5). May they not be lost or in vain. (Romans 8:28). You are amazing as you use the events of my past to make something new and beautiful—even a useful history lesson. I simply bring you my ashes and tears as that is what I have, but you give new life and peaceful joy.

Lord, I have asked to hear your voice and you use the birds to sing your love songs to me. Thank you for letting me hear them. I seek your face this morning; I see trees budding and some blossoms and I see you. You are alive and active. Thank you. I want to sense your presence and the sun is just beginning to show from behind the morning clouds on the horizon. Again, thank you—you are omnipresent!

My service is insignificant; but I love, praise, and give you thanks as you bind Satan from me and my house.

— *Day 23* —

Lord, thank you for this TAG and your reassurance that I can bring and entrust every detail of my life to you. Not only am I thankful that you love and care for me, I am also especially thankful you are the "Big 4 O*." (Psalm 36:7-9).

This a.m. I realized I am like the disciples (Luke 17:5) because I have asked you over and over to grow my faith. Though I am familiar with the verse, this morning I heard your rebuke in verse 6. I have asked as they did because I thought I needed more faith to be obedient—to do the big, impossible things with ease. Big impossible things like "forgive others"!!! I don't want to struggle! And yet, it was a struggle for you to carry the cross to Calvary!

In reality, Lord, you have already given me the faith I need to forgive myself and others. And, as I rely on you each step I take, you will give me what I need to be obedient. I need to submit and take the step.

Each day I reaffirm my decision to serve you (Joshua 24:15) so the parable you gave the disciples applies to me. (Luke 17:7-10). A servant coming in from the field doesn't sit down and eat; he first prepares dinner for his master. He doesn't expect to be thanked or asked to dine with the master. He is just to keep doing what a servant is supposed to do.

Faith is seen in obedience each day—day by day—and obedience is not a glamorous word. But, you have given me enough faith for today. Forgive me for expecting special leverage with the Father...for wanting no inconveniences, just ease and comfort. Thank you for help with self-control (Galatians 6:23) to will myself to obey.

My love, praise, and thanks are at your feet.

*Omnipotent, Omniscient, Omnipresent, and the Omega.

— *Day 24* —

Lord, that day so long ago—the day I professed that I believed you were the Son of God who shed your blood on the cross for me was a wonderful day. But, your faithfulness to me throughout the next seventy-plus years is even more wonderful. Your grace is beyond measure.

Lord, you know my testimony is not just about the day I accepted you; it is about my complete journey with you—the ups and downs. It's about the real relationship, not just knowing your name. It's about my love for you, but it is also about the times I was "Judas and betrayed you." It's about how you redeemed me from my shame and welcomed me back with those loving "everlasting arms."

Lord, I found GRACE—**G**od's **R**iches **A**t **C**hrist's **E**xpense. Help me show others that grace. Help me be a participant in someone else's story of redemption—use me!

Cleanse me. Remove any pride, envy, self-righteousness, greed—anything that would mar my relationship with you and my testimony of how wonderful you are.

Thank you for wiping out my sins and for the season of refreshing that I find in your presence now. (Acts 3:19-20).

My decision is to serve you and I lift up my house for your protection.

— *Day 25* —

Lord, I come this morning with the same thought "thank you-help me." I don't write so you'll know what I think or need; you already know. I write to remind myself of our time together. I don't ever want to forget your unconditional love, your faithfulness, and the cost of that to you.

Lord, you know I follow current events closely and often it makes me sad, frustrated, even anxious. I see our nation saying "it's okay to do the things you clearly say is sin." It's a dark, scary place out there—and, without you, that's where I would be—in the darkness.

Knowing your truth keeps me from hiding from the world and reminds me that as a believer, I must tell others—show others—just how wonderful you are. You tell me I am to be a light "glowing in the night for all the world to see," (Matthew 5:14-16), but not for my glory but so others will praise the Father.

Only in you, with you, can I even consider telling others—letting my light shine—the light that comes from you. By myself I am nothing. You give me strength and power to be and do what you have for me to do. Alone I am afraid I'll be hurt in the darkness. You hold me with your right hand—the power hand—and tell me not to fear. (Isaiah 41:13). You never change, your power never wanes, you never let go of me. Thank you.

Today, this day, may my light shine reflecting you wherever I am. I do love, praise, and honor you.

— *Day 26* —

Lord, I will never know why I have been so blessed in this life—with material blessings—but more importantly, why I was blessed with parents and family that told me of your inexplicable love for me.

Lord, when I see a broken, tattered, dirty person on the street—totally undesirable—maybe alone and unable to change their circumstances, I am reminded "I am that person except for the grace of God." From God's perspective, I am hardly desirable. Yet, I am called "beautiful, wanted, and loved (Isaiah 62:4) and you promise to redeem me as your own precious bride.

Inside that street person beats a heart that has the same needs I have—a need for you, your love, and your robe of righteousness. We— that person and I—live worlds apart; how can I show him/her how much you love them and that they too can be called "your delight."

Lord, your mandate is clear and unwavering, I am to "go and make disciples." You don't exclude anyone. I want to do that with each step I take and wherever I am. May I intentionally follow that commission in every conversation so you are glorified.

I love you and want to be of service. (Joshua 24:15). All praise and honor go to you.

— *Day 27* —

Lord, today I again thank you for this TAG; this time is one of my most cherished blessings. Nothing is more important than spending time with you, the King of kings. It is here you transform me by renewing my mind (Romans 12:2) and it here you reveal your will for my life to me .

May I just be still and know you are God and enjoy your presence. I truly want you to be my First Love (Revelation 2:4) —the ultimate desire of my heart. I am forever grateful you gave me parents, grandparents, and friends who told me about you and your sacrifice for me. You are my hope of glory. (Colossians 1:27). Yes, that is a mystery; why would you love the likes of me?

During a desperate time at the Alamo (yes, I am now Texan), Col. Wm. Travis challenged 189 soldiers to step across the line and fight to the end. They knew their fate. Missionaries have left with all their belongings in wooden boxes that would become their coffins to serve you. And, I must step across the line and take up "my cross daily and follow you," or I cannot be your disciple. (Luke 14:27).

May I today—all day—have the courage to step across the line, pick up my cross, and live in such a way that reveals I am undeniably your child, your disciple, and a "light in this world."

Lord, I love you and praise you and reaffirm my Joshua 24:15 decision.

— *Day 28* —

Lord, thank you for your gentle but vivid way you reveal a sin or sins in me that I have not yet asked forgiveness for. I want to be receptive and open in my innermost being to be filled with your fruit. (Galatians 5:22-23). And I want to be attentive to you in all my moments because in you there is peace. (Isaiah 26:3).

Again today I am asking you to take control of my tongue. That day I knew the words that came out of my mouth were caustic and unbending, but they just kept flowing—they kept on rushing out. That kid had taken 15-20 minutes of my time over and over again by being late to open the pool so I could swim, and this morning it was 30 minutes. And he didn't seem to care—or even be aware. I "smothered/drowned him with words of scorn and condemnation."

Today your Word (Luke 6:45) revealed to me the condition of my heart that day. "For the mouth speaks from the overflow of the heart." I can't make amends to that kid; but I can come to you asking forgiveness. Then I ask for more: transform my heart by renewing my mind (Romans 12:2) and control my tongue.

Help me embrace all the ways you expose sin in my life. Instead of my giving into temptation and glossing over sin, help me confess and grow as you show me the person I really am.

I want to be an equipped servant or an armed soldier (Ephesians 6:10-18) and of use to you. (Joshua 24:15). I love you, Lord.

— *Day 29* —

Lord, thank you for today, your Holy Spirit within me, and your Word. Thank you most of all for that day on Calvary and for the empty grave. You made me perfect that day (Hebrews 10:14) and you continue to set me apart for special use as I walk with you.

Thank you for not giving up on me. Help me deliberately apply your Word to every area of my life (10:16)—accepting your discipline and guidance—giving you control of today, tomorrow, and forever. Thank you for not remembering my sins (10:17); they are forgiven and forgotten. Thank you for the restoration and the growth I am experiencing today.

May I go deeper into your Word and see more and more of our Father's true nature and character. When I begin to fear or feel guilt and shame, forgive me. Help me see that fear, guilt, shame are Satan's lies that I am beginning to believe. I must remember Satan is a thief and a liar and you are the holy Son of God who offers me abundant life! (John 10:10).

Help my realization of the depth and height of your love grow. (Ephesians 3:17-19). How can I not trust someone who loves me enough to die for me! I choose to trust you, serve you, and live for you in ways that others will learn of your love.

You have my love, praise and thanks, Lord!

— *Day 30* —

Lord, thank you for allowing me this time where I find peace being in your immediate presence. Before I got out of bed this morning you had a plan for my day—one that would give me opportunity after opportunity to learn your ways and grow closer to you.

"When I look for you wholeheartedly, I will find you." (Jeremiah 29:13) and I can come to you in confidence that you will love and care for me. In you, Lord, I have God's presence and grace. You will never let go of me; therefore nothing will break my fellowship with God.

When trouble comes and Satan attacks, I will simply plant both feet firmly on the ground and say to him with assurance, "My Daddy's bigger than you and your daddy." "My God's got this." One of my favorites, Lord, from your Word is, "And my God will supply all my needs according to his riches in glory in Christ Jesus." (Philippians 4:19). Paul had been beaten and was in prison as he affirms this truth: "You have unlimited resources."

Thank you for being continually at work in my life, providing for me, protecting me, growing me. Knowing your love has no limits, I can trust your abiding presence and faithfulness.

Joshua 24:15 is my commitment. And, yes, I love and praise you as I give thanks.

— *Day 31* —

Lord, thank you for the peace you bring—you give—when I am alone and aware of your presence. That very first Sunday after you arose, your disciples were locked in a room afraid. (John 20:19) When you entered the room, just your presence as you stood there with them brought them peace. They could see you were victorious.

Lord, often I have been figuratively "locked in by fear." Thank you for allowing me to know you are with me—to be with you—to know you are victorious—to have peace with you.

When you are able to put the stars in the skies and to know everything about me and still love me, why should I be concerned about anything? That whole idea of your being "so big, so knowledgeable, so caring" is beyond my understanding, but I believe it because it is true. I now just want to apply it day after day in every area of my life.

Again today, instead of asking you to grow my trust or increase my faith, I am asking you to give me a greater awareness of just how deep and wide your love really is. And, Lord, thank you that your love is constant—it never ceases. I am never out of your presence. WOW!!!

The more intimately I experience you, the more convinced I become of your goodness—that you are the Living One who sees me and longs for me to have the abundant life that you provide to all who love you.

Let your love flow through me—use me.

— *Day 32* —

"Put off your old self, which is being corrupted by its deceitful desires; to be made new in the attitude of your minds; and ... put on the new self, created to be like God in true righteousness and holiness." (Ephesians 4:22b-24).

If I want to have lasting change in my life, I have to start with my body, and that includes changing the way I think so that I honor God through the things I think and through the things I let into my mind.

I notice that there's "a taking off and a putting on." My health really comes down to stopping some stuff I need to stop doing and starting some stuff I need to start doing. Stop putting negative, hurtful things into my body, and start putting in things that edify.

Stop putting negative, hurtful things into my mind, and start watching and listening to things that edify Jesus and make me more like him. In the renewal of my mind, I've got to put off before I can put on.

If I go to a department store to look for a new coat and find one, I then take it into one of those little changing rooms. If I'm wearing a coat already, I don't go in there and put the new coat on over my old coat. That would be silly, because I'm not going to know if it fits! It makes sense to take off the old one before I put on the new one.

Lord, help me see that that's true spiritually and emotionally and mentally, too. I've got to take off the old before I can put on the new one. Lord, I want you to make me new each day by renewing my mind. (Romans 12:2).

I am yours; use me as you will.

— *Day 33* —

"No eye has ever seen, no ear has heard, and no mind has imagined what God has prepared for those who love him. (1 Corinthians 2:9b).

As a child, living about 50 miles north of Memphis, TN, I would see pictures in the Commercial Appeal of women dressed in gorgeous gowns and men in tuxes, and the gala affairs as the Queen of Cotton was crowned. I would try to imagine what all that would be like and mama would try to explain the festivities to me; but the experiences I had on a dirt farm in Northeast Arkansas were no base for comprehending what she was saying. She might as well have been speaking in Chinese. It was a waste of time.

I think the same is true of heaven. Lord, I cannot compare heaven to anything I've experienced on earth. Earth is not even a poor copy of eternity. In heaven I will be with you and every person I've ever known who believed in you, loved, and followed you.

Your Word mentions rewards in heaven. I just have to decide where I want to be rewarded—on this temporary side of eternity or on the side that lasts forever.

I think I will work in heaven (Luke 16:10-12). I think I will use my God-given shape—whatever that is—to do what I love to do. There will be rest as well. My work will be a restful joy—not a burden.

In your Word, Matthew tells me there will be rejoicing in heaven. (25:21). All of us are going to celebrate. We will enjoy being with God and you, Lord, and with one another. That heavenly party is going to last an eternity. Although my understanding of heaven is not any more clear than was the childish picture I had of all the activities happening during the Cotton Festival in Memphis, heaven's party is one I don't want to miss! I hope I see all of my friends there!

— *Day 34* —

Lord, thank you for loving me and never giving up on me! Never let me give up on anyone else. Help me love each one of your children as you want them loved. If you are trying to teach me something here in this situation, help me learn it quickly.

Lord, I have to go back to my basic premise. If it is happening, you have given your permission; otherwise, it would not be happening. And, if it is okay with you, it has to be okay with me. Who am I to think I know more than you? Since it is happening, teach me what you want me to learn or show me what you want me to do. How do you want me to glorify you here?

Romans 8:28 is as true today as it was when Paul wrote it. I believe it to my very core; but sometimes it is still terribly painful. But I know that all that happens to us/me is working for our/my good if we/I love God—and I do—and am fitting into his plans. Yes, Lord, I want to fit into your plans.

Lord, some situations are almost too painful to bear. I am not angry with that person—or those people, I am angry that Satan has such a hold in this situation...but I know you are omnipotent and victorious. Maybe I am angry because I can't understand the thinking....maybe I am not supposed to understand. But, I know others are hurting too. Give each of us strength, courage, patience, love, and unity as we go through this step by step. We can know your presence with us; and, Lord, strengthen each of our relationships. Hold each of us close in your arms.

Lord, hear my cries to you tonight. Guard and protect us all. Guide each of us. Bind Satan from my family that we may serve and glorify you.

Yes, Romans 8:28 is still true.

— *Day 35* —

Lord, I come to you again thanking you for your presence with me. I am asking the Holy Spirit to guide me as I read your Word; I want to continue to build my life on its divine truth. I want to meditate on it, find joy in it, learn from it, come closer and live in obedience to you through it. I am seeking you with my whole heart. I want to diligently and faithfully live the way you want me to live.

Am I selfish, Lord? Your Word tells me I will be happy/blessed when I walk in an "undefiled way" (Psalm 119:1-8). I want to be happy and blessed. I want the joy that only you can give. I want to live free from the devastating effects of sin. I need your Holy Spirit to be a guide for understanding and a help for following your laws. I need your Primer for my daily conduct; I want to serve and honor you.

Thank you for your assurance that I will be able to come to you without shame when I follow your Word. You expect me to be obedient in every area of my life, but I know I will not be able to do that without the Holy Spirit's help. I want to be obedient and in that joyous relationship with you, Lord. You took my shame to the cross and left it there; I don't want to add more shame now in this late stage of my life.

Just learning your Word, seeking your face, looking for guidance is a form of my praise and worship. It is my attempt to have an "upright heart." (7). David makes a definite commitment to keep your "statutes" as he pleads with you not to forsake him. (8). I understand that need for assurance.

I know I want to be with you without shame; I want to follow your Word, but I fail you often; I need you desperately, Lord.

Help me hear the Holy Spirit who is the master-teacher of your Word— and learn. (John 14:23-26).

I love, praise and honor you with my desire to serve you.

— *Day 36* —

Lord, you are holy, supreme, sovereign and worthy of my complete, submissive obedience and praise. Thank you and thank you for your Word—the one source for all the information I really need to live life well in the fullness you intended.

Satan is always out there tempting me to live according to worldly desires and to wander away from you. With my whole heart, I want your Word in me so I don't sin against you, Lord. (Psalm 119:9-16). Cleanse me. Purify me. Let your Word guide, guard, and protect me so that I live within the truth you provide.

Lord, I don't need more facts and information from your Word; I need you. (v.12). I want to learn from you, allowing the Holy Spirit to teach me. (2 Peter 1:19-21). Lord, I want my praise and worship to be dynamic and open. (Matthew 7:28-29). I want your Word to continue to change me to be more like you. (Ephesians 4:23-24).

Lord, I write to reinforce on my heart and in my mind the truth that I find in your Word. I want to repeat it to myself allowing my ears to add additional reinforcement. David says he is speaking what he learned from you. (v.13).

Lord, help me! I want to live and apply your Word in my life so others can see you. I want others to see the joy I find in you, (v. 14-16) and I will not forget your Word.

I love my TAG—my time aware of your presence.

— *Day 37* —

I thank you for meeting with me for a TAG. I want to be open and honest with you. I tell you I want to be merciful. Who am I kidding? The Good Samaritan modeled mercy when he reached out to care for the injured man lying at the side of the road. There's always a cost to kindness and mercy and a sacrifice in service. Look what it cost you!

Showing mercy usually requires a sacrifice of time, energy, money, and possibly a reputation. The Samaritan took the injured man to a hotel. He likely had to walk a great distance, because he put the man on his donkey. He took care of him through the night, he provided for his needs, and then he even paid the bill—all at his own personal expense. He didn't just call the authorities. He did all he could to help.

And what did he have to gain from his service? Nothing! He just did it out of compassion. And that's the kind of service you and God, the Father, want from me.

Your Word even promises that when I help hurting people by giving what I have, I will be blessed in return. Lord, your Word says, "Feed the hungry, and help those in trouble. Then your light will shine out from the darkness, and the darkness around you will be as bright as noon. The Lord will guide you continually, giving you water when you are dry and restoring your strength. You will be like a well-watered garden, like an ever-flowing spring." (Isaiah 58:10-11).

With promises like that, is it that I don't trust your Word when I am not more willing to be merciful and offer grace?

Mercy will cost me time, money, or potentially relationships. Mercy that doesn't cost much isn't worth much, but whatever cost I incur to demonstrate mercy will be worth it. Help me live that out. I do love you, Lord.

— *Day 38* —

Thank you for another TAG. Your Word tells me, "Never walk away from someone who deserves help; your hand is God's hand for that person. Don't tell your neighbor, 'Maybe some other time' or 'Try me tomorrow' when the money's right there in your pocket." (Proverbs 3:27-28 MSG).

Your Word is telling me to seize the moment. Don't wait, don't delay, and don't procrastinate. Do what I can at this moment. Love is not so much something I feel as it is something I do.

The Samaritan took action. He stooped down and got on the injured man's level. He didn't act superior. He used what he had: wine to disinfect and oil to soothe the wounds—the best medication of the day. He probably used his own clothes to bandage this guy's wounds. After all, he's not a doctor; he didn't have a medicine cabinet with him. He just served. He did the best he could with what he had.

Wow, Lord, you are saying "Don't wait for better conditions. When you call me to minister to somebody, you want it done NOW! When you show me a need, you want me to meet it NOW!

I am weak and fearful, but I must be willing to take a risk. I must be willing to be interrupted. To be a servant I must move against my fears. The Samaritan may have had fears like: Are robbers still in the area? Is this a trap? Will he accept my help? What if I can't help him? What will others say?

I often don't want to get involved with other people's pain and brokenness because it reminds me of my own. But, mercy moves in spite of fear. Your mercy touched me when I was untouchable and loved me when I was unlovable. Help me live out your Word in my life. I do love you and thank you for your mercy to me.

— *Day 39* —

Lord, there are people in my life that drive me nuts; they are EGRs— acronym for Extra Grace Required. Am I an EGR to you? Did you put those EGRs in my life to be heavenly sandpaper? They irritate me, but are you using them to smooth my rough edges and reshape my character? If so, thank you!

Some EGRs are minor irritations. They may drive too slowly in the passing lane. Some of them may be more challenging. They critique my every action. Other EGRs may be just plain mean. They never appreciate anything. They can be rude and negative, demanding, demeaning, and disapproving. No one could make them happy. Whatever is done, it's not good enough.

Help me show mercy when I'd rather show those EGRs the door. Help me look behind their behavior and see their pain. I know, Lord, when people are hurting others, it's because they're hurting on the inside. Hurt people hurt people; they may be full of fear and insecurity. They are probably dealing with pain and pressure I know nothing about.

Whether it's a fight with their spouse, kid or kids with problems, financial troubles, health issues, or just any thorn in their side that's causing them to be mean to everyone around them, help me look past their behavior and offer the extra grace that's needed to glorify you— even if I never understand the situation.

Your Word tells me, "When a fool is annoyed, he quickly lets it be known. Smart people will ignore an insult." (Proverbs 12:16). Help me see the pain behind their behavior. Only then—with your strength, your wisdom, and your love—will I be able to ignore their insults. Help me, Lord. I want to be like you, responding with love and grace. Thank you for the EGRs in my life; may they be my teachers.

— *Day 40* —

Lord, I am particularly thankful for these last 40 days and the TAGs I have had with you.

I haven't heard your voice, but I have sensed your answers to my requests. Just one example is that I have asked you for wisdom and discernment, and I find your message: "A person's wisdom yields patience; it is to one's glory to overlook an offense." (Proverbs 19:11). I have a choice on how to respond to any situation and the one you recommend most often is to respond with mercy and grace. You also tell me to "Watch my words and hold my tongue." (Proverbs 21:23). Lord, if I will just stay close to you, listening for you, you will give me the wisdom and discernment I need. Thank you for meeting my every need. Lord, thank you for including me in your love.

Just because this special season with you is ending, I simply want to continue this focus on you, your presence, your guidance, and your understanding. I want your Spirit to grow its fruit in me. (Galatians 5:22-23).

There isn't a problem that I face that you haven't experienced; so I am continuing to ask you to "make me wise in spiritual things and teach me how to live in ways that please and honor you." (1 Colossians 1:9). May I always do good, kind things for others and at the same time get to know you better and better.

Without you, I am nothing. Joshua 24:15 is still my mantra. And I still need to call on your name and your power to bind Satan from me and my family.

Yes, Lord, I do repeat myself often; but I love you, I praise you, I thank you. I am in your debt.

Again, Lord,
I Repeat

— *Beginning* —

Thank you, Lord, for this day and this particular time with you. As I seek you and study your Word, help me see your plan and know that you orchestrate events to draw me closer to you. I want to know you more deeply and see "your perspective." Even when the circumstances aren't as I would like, I want to rest on your promise that you are always with me. (Romans 8:38-39).

Your promises are there; maybe not in my hand, but always within my reach! (Hebrews 10:23). And you are faithful.

This alone time with you is not a luxury, but an essential! It is here that I come to be equipped for the day; and I need all of your armor. (Ephesians 6:12:18). I submit to you, Lord, asking for your power to bind Satan from me and my family—each of us. (James 4:7-8).

As I plan for the day—limited as my activities are, teach me to hold them lightly and be ready to alter them to please you. The most important thing for me is to determine and take the "next right step" now.

Lord, forgive me of all my sins—the ones I see and those I have yet to see. I love, praise, and honor you and my decision is made: Joshua 24:15.

— *Day 2* —

Lord, my decision is made: Joshua 24:15 is my commitment to serve you. That's what my mind says; but, Lord, I am trying to figure out how to do that in "real life"—day after day. Teach me. Show me. Then, Lord, I need strength and courage to do that. I want to learn to live in dependence on you—totally!

Maybe I am like Gideon—hiding down in the winepress threshing wheat! (Judges 6 through 9). But, I want to learn how "to be changed" from a "scaredy cat" to an idol fighter. That had to be an exciting adventure! Then to go to battle against thousands with only 300 men—when it is the enemy who has the swords and shields! That has to be faith and trust. How did he get from the oppressed victim in the winepress to victor?

You have not changed! You are the same God today as you were then! Your promises are for me today just as they were for Gideon, David, Esther, Miriam, and the others back then. I want to learn what you want me to learn about you from Gideon, et al. After three chapters in Judges (6-9), he is not mentioned again until Paul says, "It would take too long to tell all about Gideon's faith...he trusted God, won battles, overthrew the enemy, ruled well, and received the promises of God."

Help me, Lord, to learn to walk in trust and faith like that. As far as me and my house, we will serve you. Bind Satan—in all his disguises— from me and each of my family so that we may be a glory to you. My love, praise, and honor go to you, Lord.

— *Day 3* —

Lord, again, thank you for this time with you. Thank you for all that you are—sovereign, love, peace, joy, patient, kind, good, faithful, gentle, and self-controlled (Galatians 5:22-23) to mention a few. Lord, I want that fruit to grow in me. I want to be like you. You and the Father created me and your Spirit lives in me. May your light shine through me so others see you and have hope.

I keep thinking about this "living in dependence on you." As I learn to depend more and more on you, may I be more open to your working in my life. I want to see the miracles that are happening—as miracles—not just "coincidences." Lord, I don't think you have stopped performing miracles; I think I have been just too blind to see them. "Open my eyes that I might see the glimpses of truths you have for me." (Hymn).

Lord, I read your Word and I say to myself, "I want to be like Gideon, David, Joshua, Esther, or other spiritual giants mentioned in your Word that I am focused on." Forgive me! You made me to be Lee and in your image. Help me be the person you created me to be, accepting who I am today and growing in faith and trust to be the person you want me to be tomorrow. "Your grace is sufficient for me" as I am at this moment. (2 Corinthians 12:9-10). It is in you that I live, move, and have my being. (Acts 17:28). I am thankful that you live in me and promise never to leave me. (John 14:20).

You know my concerns for this nation—its people and its leaders. I leave them in your care. I don't know the needs of each of my family—except we all need a close walk with you. I ask that for me and for them now. Bind Satan from us.

I love, praise, and honor you as I reaffirm my decision of Joshua 24:15.

— *Day 4* —

Lord, I so glad you allow me into your presence again this morning to be refreshed and prepared for the day.

Lord, I don't have any difficulty accepting you as the God/Man; Son of God. You came, walked this earth, died on the cross shedding your blood for my sins, were buried and after three days rose from the grave, then later ascended into heaven. I accept that even though I don't understand it all. I accept God the Father—again, even if I don't understand it all. I can pray to either or both of you in my heart, soul, and mind.

Now, Lord, I am really trying to grasp the Holy Spirit—the counselor and comforter—who came to live in me the day I became a believer. Am I asking for the wrong thing when I ask to be attuned to the Holy Spirit? You are three in one—the Trinity. Is it your Spirit that guides me, gives me discernment? Is it just semantics?

Lord, I don't want to miss out on 1/3 of what you have for me. I want to know all of you: God, the Father—God, the Son—God, the Holy Spirit. (Deuteronomy 4:29). I am not doubting your presence; I have felt it. Maybe I'm not supposed to "understand." Is this the part I am to accept on faith? Grow my faith in you, Lord, and my understanding of you. I am yours. I love, praise, and honor you. I want to serve you as you want me to. Joshua 24:15 is my prayer. Hold all of us—me and each of my family, your church, this nation—close to you.

— *Day 5* —

Lord, I have so much to be thankful for. The list is miles long, but I am most thankful for this quiet peace I find when I come to you in these early morning hours. I am safe and secure; you are my hiding place and my protection. (Psalm 32:7). Here I am energized and equipped for anything this day offers—pleasures, difficulties, adventures, disappointments.

Here you remind me that you are not only my King, you are also my Friend! You laid down your life for me—shedding your blood that I could live with you forever. (John 15:13-15). You are with me now and will be on into heaven. Lord, is it the Holy Spirit that helps me stay conscious of you?

The Trinity—the 3 in 1—If it is the Holy Spirit that I am "in tune with," am I attuned to you and the Father at the same time? Lord, you can see my mind has difficulty grasping the whole picture.

Lord, maybe I don't need to understand. You know that I love you, want to please you, and yet still fail you so often. I know I am satisfied with you and all that you are. I just want to know you more fully—and I don't want to miss anything you have for me just because I didn't ask.

Today, I love you, praise you, honor you! Forgive me as I fail you and fail to stay close to you. May I be the channel you use to bless others today. Joshua 24:15 is my prayer and all my cares are yours.

— *Day 6* —

Lord, I know it is repetitive, but I must say it again, "Thank you for who you are and for being with me this a.m." Better still, thank you for allowing me this time in your intimate presence.

"Be still and know that I am God." (Psalm 46:10). Lord, you are sovereign and I want to know you more each day. I want to be so still that I hear you plainly and truly sense your leading. It is in you that I have a sense of well being; it is in you that I am refreshed and revitalized. I rest in the fact that nothing can separate me from your love. (Romans 8:38-39).

Live through me, Lord. Let my mouth, my hands, and my feet serve you—be yours. May my eyes and ears see and hear what there is that you want me to do. You are the "Vine" and I am only "a branch," (John 15:5) and apart from you, I can do nothing of eternal value.

Thank you for giving me free will, but I want you to transform me so that I know what your "good, perfect, pleasing will" is. I don't want to conform to the pattern of this world. (Romans 12:2). Help me give thanks to you when those I love and care about are using their free will in ways that I find repulsive. I'm sure you have been repulsed by the sins I have committed and are not happy with me when I choose not to search for your will in and for my life; forgive me.

This day may I be strong in you and in your power. (Ephesians 6:10-18). I am yours. Love, praise, honor belong to you. Joshua 24:15 is my decision for me and each of my house.

— *Day 7* —

Lord, thank you for this "out-in-the-open, early-morning" time with you. Experiencing your handiwork is reason enough to trust you. Lord, I want to "put you on" and "wear you" throughout this day. I want to think your thoughts. (Romans 13:14). Only in you am I equipped to face whatever people or situations you have for me today. May I be compassionate, kind, humble, gentle, and patient—in your power, not mine. (Colossians 3:12).

Lord, you are the God of abundance, and I know you will meet my needs according to your glorious riches. (Philippians 4:19). And again, Lord, never let me twist your Word like a spoiled child saying, "But, Daddy, you said so and so." Help me understand your Word as you want me to know it.

I have failed you often—and continue to fail you, but I am clothed in that luxurious "robe of righteousness. (Isaiah 61:10). I know I will never be great or do anything great; but let me be a blessing to others in your strength. May your fruit (Galatians 5:22-23) grow in me for your glory.

Our nation and its leaders desperately need you, Lord. May each of us draw closer to you—seeking your face.

Love, honor, praise, and thanksgiving belong to you.

— *Day 8* —

Lord, I thank you for your blessings—which are too numerous to list. I don't know why you have been so gracious to me—giving me spiritual, emotional, physical, and financial blessings. But, I thank you!! I love, praise, and honor you for who you are. And, I pray that I would be like Habakkuk (3:17-19)—and praise, honor, trust you even though I were stripped of everything. I pray I would love you just because you are a loving, good God.

Lord, help me accept this day exactly as it happens! I want to trust you absolutely, completely! I want to rest in your sovereignty and your faithfulness! May I be called an "oak of righteousness that you have planted for yourself." (Isaiah 61:3).

Lord, help me grow in you! May I desire "growth in you." May I be ready for you to "grow me." I know growth can be painful. Help me not be resistant to it. As I am refreshed and revitalized in your presence, teach me. Put your thoughts into my mind. Show me what is important and what is not. You are the author of peace, not confusion. (1 Corinthians 14:33).

No matter where I am in this world, I know I am not beyond your loving presence. You are not too deaf to hear me and your arm is long enough to reach me and strong enough to hold me. (Isaiah 59:1).

Joshua 24:15 is my decision again today. Bind Satan from me and my house so we can serve and be a glory to you.

— *Day 9* —

Lord, I trust you. Help me trust you more. I love and thank you. Help me. Isn't that how I start 99% of everything I say to you? Help me welcome challenging times as opportunities to trust you and see that you are faithful. (James 1:2). When I read your Word telling me to "Consider it pure joy when I face trials," I can do that when it is "someone else's trials." I must grow in trust before I can consider it joy when the trials are my trials.

I can say I believe your "good and perfect" Word...and mean it; but living it out is beyond me at this point in my walk with you. Raise my trust level, Lord. Maybe Paul was growing to that point when he says, "I have learned the secret to contentment" in Philippians 4:12 and then follows with "I can do all things God asks me to do" in 4:13. He was in prison as he makes those statements. I wonder!

Lord, I am a wimp. You have been so gracious to me and you have asked so little of me. I pray that I will stand firm—praising you—when *my* troubled times comes. And, if I haven't become strong in you "by then," I pray I will just hold tightly to your hand, depending on you and you alone, giving thanks with each breath that I take.

"You will keep me in perfect peace when I am steadfast and trusting you." (Isaiah 26:3). Today is yours. I want to live it in a way that pleases you. My decision is Joshua 24:15. Love, honor, praise, and thanksgiving belong to you.

— Day 10 —

Lord, I am so thankful you are with me. Today there is no activity on my schedule that has any eternal value—in fact very little activity "scheduled" at all. There's feed the dogs, water the plants, pick up the Andrews' paper, but not a thing involving another human being!

No one would notice if I did—or did not—show up for lunch, dinner, or breakfast tomorrow. I'm not on the "pity pot;" I am just saying how I see things are at this moment. And I am okay! Is this a small part of what Paul is referring to in Philippians 4:12?

I am here in your presence. I know you care about the sparrow. (Matthew 6:26). I know I can never be separated from your love. (Romans 8: 38-39). Though I feel alone; I know I am not alone. I want to write your Word—your promises—on my heart so that I am filled with joy and peace and so that I will not sin against you! (Isaiah 54:10, Genesis 28:15, Matthew 28:10). Lord, I would like to wrap myself in your Word. Write your Word on the back of my eyelids so I am reminded of them at all times.

I love, praise, and honor you as I say "Thank you for all that you are and for all the blessings you provide." Joshua 24: 15 continues to be my motto!

— *Day 11* —

Lord, thank you for your omnipresence! And thank you for being immutable! Everything around me changes—except you! You are always present and you are always the same—yesterday, today, and forever. It is in that reality that I can rejoice. (Philippians 4:4). Your love is constant regardless of the circumstances.

Lord, I wonder would I have felt that way, made that statement years ago when the Twin Towers were destroyed and as 3000 people died around me. I pray that I would have. Paul was in prison (Philippians 4:12) when he talks about contentment in any situation.

Sin and evil are in this world—because Adam and Eve chose to rebel! It flourishes today because we choose to rebel. Lord, you knew when you gave us moral freedom, we would rebel! Yet you loved us enough to give us that choice. Lord, I want to submit to you and live in that "love relationship" with you—to know your presence in every circumstance.

Lord, I want to learn submission! I want to recognize your voice, see your leadership, and be obedient.

Joshua 24:15 is my fervent prayer! Hold each of us close to you so that we may be a reflection of you and your love. Bind Satan from our lives.

Our national and state leaders, courts, cities, churches, families all need you desperately. May you be head of it all. My love, honor, and praises are to you.

— *Day 12* —

Lord, you know my first cup of coffee is important to me, but sharing it with you makes it "more so." This fresh day you have for me is reason to rejoice! In this moment there is peace—even if the dog barks and a car horn blasts. In you, there is peace! John 14:27 is for me today.

And Lord, as I read Isaiah 30:15, I want to stop before I get to the last phrase or rewrite the verse and say "I want repentance and rest in you and the strength that comes as I trust you." (Lord, don't let me be out of line saying that; your Word is perfect and no disrespect is intended.) I want to know you more, be constantly aware of you, and see you in every encounter.

Lord, forgive me for my criticism of your servant. Right now, I pray your servant will look to you for guidance and strength, that he will be the leader of your church as you want him to be, and that he will be all you want him to be. Forgive me, Lord, for not bringing my concerns to you—instead of taking them to someone who is not charge. Bind Satan from me and from your church. Lord, control my tongue! Let it be used to praise, honor, and glorify you.

I cannot retrieve the words I spoke, but I am asking you to put them under the "cloak you gave me" and "Let the words of my mouth and the meditations of my heart be acceptable to you."

Joshua 24:15 is my decision this morning for me and my family.

— *Day 13* —

Lord, I want to be aware you are the Creator—my Creator. You are King of kings and I am your subject. You are the Potter and I am clay. (Romans 9:20-21). You are my Shepherd and I want to know your voice. I am not your equal; but you allow me to walk with you, holding your hand. Lord, let me reword that to "walk hand in hand." It is your mighty hand that holds me secure.

Help me learn acceptance: acceptance of both circumstances and people exactly as they are at this moment. My responsibility—as I understand it—is to love the people and glorify you. Help me not judge. (Matthew 7:1). You are sovereign. If it were your divine will for things—people—to be different today, they would be different today! These circumstances and people may be for the purpose of teaching me or drawing me closer to you. If that is so, help me learn what you want me to learn! Quickly! You bring things on your own time. (Timothy 6:15).

Lord, I know that you just saw once again what I just did: I was telling you—do it "Quickly!" Forgive me and help me learn "Acceptance."

I want to remain focused on YOU this day as I go about my activities. I want to be aware of your presence. You never change.

Love, honor, and praise are due you. Bind Satan from me and my house—that we may glorify you. Joshua 24:15.

— *Day 14* —

Thank you for today! Thank you for the assurance that I am safe and secure in your presence—and that you care for and guard each of those I love. You are with me now and will be all the way to heaven where I will see you Face to face. (1 Corinthians 13:12). That will be joy untold, but until then I will hold onto your promise to never leave me or forsake me. (Joshua 1:5).

Help me be consciously aware of your presence throughout the day. Help me reflect your love to others in ways that they will see "*YOU*" and not "me."

Thank you for the worldly blessings you have given and continue to give me: health, family, friends, resources, and the list never ends. And, especially, thank you for that "robe of righteousness" that I didn't deserve and cost you so much. (Isaiah 61:10). Help me love you more than the blessings you give.

You know what my cares are for each one of my family. Each day I lay those cares at your feet; help me trust you enough to leave them there. I just seem to go back, pick them up, and interfere with your plan. Forgive me for trying to "do things my way." Forgive me, Lord, for not trusting you. I seem to forget you don't have grandchildren; each of us is your child. And, you love each one of them just as you love me. Thank you.

— *Day 15* —

Lord, I lift you up in praise and bless your name. I constantly boast about what God can do, is doing and will do. (Psalm 44:8). I can never thank you enough, Lord. (Psalm 66:4). All the earth will worship you (Psalm 68:32) and sing your praise. (Psalm 84:4). I am happy when I praise you; and if my voice were melodic, I would sing songs of praise. (Psalm 143:6). My only hope is you and in you.

God, you are faithful and awesome beyond words! (Psalm 47:1-4). You bless me. (Psalm 48:4-8). You are my protector, my deliverer, and my shield. (Psalm 81:7). Trials may be to test my faith and help me grow in trust as I reach out to you. (Psalm 77:15). You redeemed me. (Psalm 68:7). You will lead me just as you led your children out of Egypt. (Psalm 76:9). You are my defender.

You never change. You are the same God for me today as you were for David. Help me become more aware of your presence with me and all that you are so that I may share your promises with others—and so that I may be strengthened. "Help me remember this moment with you" is my prayer today...as well as Joshua 24:15.

I am blessed when I believe in you, trust in you, and rely on you knowing my hope and my confidence is in you. (Jeremiah 17:7). I love you, Lord.

— *Day 16* —

Thank you for this day you have made. May I find joy in your presence wherever I go and whatever develops. You created this day; it is not a chance occurrence. You would be present even if I were not aware of your presence. (Psalm 21:6).

I want to live in unison with you—dependent on you. In you I experience peace, joy, a sense of being complete.

Help me seek you in "everything and everywhere" as if you were a hidden treasure—because you are the most precious of all treasures. Help me concentrate on keeping in step with you as you lead the way guiding me along the path you have for me to follow. Some of the places seem alien to me; help me trust you more each day.

Lord, I am back to the "4 O's." You are omnipotent, omniscient, omnipresent, and the Omega. How can I not trust you—even if the place is foreign? When I breathe deep within me that you have plans to prosper me (Jeremiah 29:11), I can relax and enjoy the moment with you.

Nothing can rob me of my inheritance—you are my hope of heaven! So, help me, Lord, stay close to you, looking for your guidance. (Proverbs 16:9). Today! Now!

I am yours—your beloved child. You bought me and the cost was dear. With that investment, I know you will continue to care for me. I love and praise you, Lord, as I pray Joshua 24: 15.

— *Day 17* —

(At Glen's) Lord, thank you again—and again—for the blessings you provide, but thank you most for being you...a constant, consistent, caring, loving, sovereign Lord and Savior.

Today help me please, serve, and glorify you in everything I say and do. May that be my focal point of this day. (Matthew 6:33). You always did what pleased your Father, and I want to be like that. (John 8:29).

Lord, I am so thankful you gave me free will, but what a huge responsibility that is. You give me choices; may I put you first in each choice I make. Let everything I do be for you whether it's pulling weeds, cleaning the bathroom, or holding the hand of one of your needy children. (Colossians 3:23-24). I want a vibrant relationship with you.

You are Immanuel and you never leave me. (Matthew 1:23). Nothing separates me from your love. (Romans 8:38-39). You know what I need more than I do—and as I lift up each of my family, the same is still true. You know what they need and you know your plan—your divine plan. May I confidently pray in submission and for submission to you and not tell you what to do.

Joshua 24:15 is still my prayer. May I leave the details to you. Bind Satan from me and each of mine. Thanks. Love. Honor. Praise. (Chimes just rang from church downtown).

— *Day 18* —

Lord, today help me live in union with you, dependent on you, know the peace you provide, and leave all my cares with you. (1 Peter 5:6-7). Lord, when I attempt to control any situation or person remind me that you are sovereign—not me. (Proverbs 16:9). I want to learn to be your instrument, to be used by you, to let your love flow through me.

When things aren't going "my way," help me be joyful in hope, patient, and faithful in prayer (Romans 12:12) submitting to your sovereignty. At times like these, I want to remember you never leave me and never let go of my hand. I want to be equipped with the "whole armor" you provide: belt of truth, breastplate of righteousness, shoes of peace, shield of faith, salvation's helmet and the sword of the Spirit. (Ephesians 6:10-18; 1 Thessalonians 5:18).

And, Lord, under this armor, may your love be in my deepest recesses and totally filling me to overflowing. It's hard to picture being fully dressed for battle and yet filled with your love. (Psalm 139:1-4 & 23-24). Am I losing it, Lord?

I am yours. I fail you often, but I am yours. My decision is Joshua 24:15. I pray that I and each of my family will serve you and glorify you. Thank you for all that you are and all that you have already done for me. Love, Honor, Praise!

— *Day 19* —

(Still at Glen's) Lord, I am really trying to expand this idea from your Word "This is the day the Lord has made and I will rejoice and be glad in it." (Psalm 118:24). I want to tell you how A.J. is hurting, that each of us needs your guidance as we find our purpose in you, and my list of cares and concerns goes on and on. You already know these things and "probably" don't me need to tell you "how to fix these situations."

Instead, I need to work on my own relationship with you; show me where and how I can strengthen it today!

I thank you for giving each of us "free will." I especially thank you that you gave it to me. Now, help me continue to give you thanks when others I care about so deeply don't exercise their "free will" like *I* think they should. Please help *me* resign from trying to be God—and forgive *me*.

Heaven and earth do intersect in my mind, and the battle goes on for control! Lord, I want to learn acceptance—knowing you made this day, you are in control, and Romans 8:28 is still a truth! (and Romans 8:6).

Thank you, Lord, for allowing me to sit here in your presence, focused on you, enjoying this privilege because I belong to you. When the world begins to bombard me, help me stay in continual communication with you. Give me protection and discernment for each encounter as you fill me with your love.

My decision is still Joshua 24:15. Forgive me when I fail...which I do so often. Love, Praise, and Honor!

— *Day 20* —

Lord, thank you for this day and let gratitude be in every fiber of my being for you have blessed me abundantly. Lord, I know you are present with me, but I want to feel your presence. I desire more of you. Write your Word on my heart just as David asked you to write on his eons ago.

Thank you for being my Lord who loves me and provides for my every need. Today I am asking you to help me prepare for Satan's attack; I want to be ready. I want my family to be ready. You recognized the devil and came to destroy his works. (1 John 3:8). You saw him fall from heaven (Luke 10:18); you know he's real, evil, and crafty. (Matthew 6:13).

I want to put on the full armor (Ephesians 6:14-18) and I am asking you to guide, provide, empower and protect me and mine as we stand against the devil—resisting his attacks.

He will try to distract our walk with you. Help us to watch, pray, and stay alert. And, he will try to deceive us. He's a liar. (John 8:44). Help me be serious and disciplined for prayer.

He will attempt to divide my family's relationships (Mark 3:25). Protect the husband/wife relationships, the parent/child relationships, the sibling relationships, etc. Help us stay focused on your will; may your Holy Spirit keep us walking in truth; and give us your patient, forgiving love for each other to unite us in you.

Yes, Lord, we need you. "The devil prowls around like a roaring lion, seeking someone to devour." Help us resist him and stay firm in you.

Lord, just cleanse me for living in this world today. I know you want to draw each of us to you so I am asking you to do that and put us in your protective care. I love and praise you.

— *Day 20 Later* —

Lord, I can't think you enough for this day, for each of your blessings. You are my strength and my song, my salvation, and my God! I will praise you and give thanks. (Exodus 15:2). Your ear is always strong enough to hear my pleas and your arm is long enough to reach me and strong enough to save me (Isaiah 59:1) so I will lay my requests before you this evening and wait patiently—hopefully I am patient—for your answer. (Psalm 5:3).

As I wait, help me be still and let your thoughts form within me. You created the universe and yet you choose to live in me, to be my counselor and my comforter. May I hear your holy whispers to me and learn your words of Life, Love, Joy, Peace.

Lord, I don't want to conform to the patterns of this world. I want to be transformed as I renew my thoughts in you. I want to know your good, pleasing, perfect will. (Romans 12:2).

Show me, even at this late hour, lead me to one person I can encourage/ lift up. Prepare me and let me be used by you. May I be a channel for your love to flow to that person. I want to walk in the light of your presence. (Psalm 89:15).

My prayer is Joshua 24:15; help me take the next right step doing that. I love, honor, and praise you!

— *Day 21* —

Today I seek your face; you are my refuge. (Psalm 71:1). And, I thank you for being here with me. The more I rest in your presence, the more I can learn of your love—the more freely I can experience you! I want to know you more. I want to grasp just how "wide, long, deep, and high" your love really is. (Ephesians 3:17-19).

Lord, at those last moments on the cross you said to your father, "Father, into your hands I entrust my spirit." Help me have that same trust—regardless of the circumstances. (Luke 23:46).

This day, even as I am involved in routine activities, help me "Be still and know you are God." (Psalm 46:10). Help me know/experience your omnipotence, omniscience, and omnipresence.

Grow your fruit (Galatians 5:22-23) in me. May I become all you created me to be. My prayer is that I and my family will serve you all the days of our lives. (Joshua 24:15).

— *Day 22* —

Lord, you are my strength and my song, you have become my salvation. You are my God (Son of God), and I will praise you. (Exodus 15:2). Help me hold unswervingly to the hope that I talk about—because you are faithful. (Hebrews 10:23). Take my every thought and make it obedient to you. (2 Corinthians 10:5). I want to totally trust you.

Thank you for continually communicating with me: (Psalm 8:14): sometimes through glorious sunsets; other times in the faces and voices of those I love; maybe a beautiful cardinal feeding at the bird feeder on the back patio; or a gentle breeze across my face. May I hear you in the depths of my spirit!

May your Spirit that lives in me sharpen my awareness of you so I can discover more of you and rejoice. Help me look and listen for you in every quiet moment. (Jeremiah 29:13...1 Corinthians 6:19 and Psalm 19:1-2).

Lord, forgive me for each failure—which happens often. Keep control of my tongue unless it is to glorify you. Show me the person(s) I am to encourage today.

May your fruit (Galatians 5:22-23) grow in me today and each day. Joshua 24:15 is my prayer and I need your guidance to take the next right step to do that. Our nation needs you and I rest on Romans 8:28. Hold us all close to you. We all matter to you!

I love, honor, praise, and thank you.

— *Day 23* —

Lord, thank you for this time alone with you. You are my glorious Lord. You are my salvation and you care for me daily just as you did for David. (Psalm 68:19). It amazes me that you love me just as you loved him! You are my shelter and my shield; I put my hope in you alone. (Psalm 119:14). You are my hiding place—a place of quiet retreat! (Psalm 32:7).

Lord, on those mornings when "I don't feel like facing the day," help me remember that your Word gives life. Even David had his mornings "in the dust." (Psalm 119:25).

You came that I could have abundant life (John 10:10) and that isn't wealth and health—that's continual dependence on you. Help me be on the lookout for what you are doing all around me; your handiwork is everywhere. You will give me strength to do what you want done in and through me. (Philippians 4: 13).

Give me a cheerful heart to lift others up. (Proverbs 17:22). Today is yours; I will rejoice in it. I love and praise you and leave my cares with you—especially for our nation, its leaders, and each of my family and friends. We are all in your hands.

— Day 24 —

Lord, help me live first and foremost in your presence. I want to become more aware of you and more aware of you in those around me. Increase my ability to give love and encouragement to those I encounter. Let your peace permeate my words and my demeanor. As I take refuge in you, may I find your joy and give thanks for your protection. (Psalm 5:11). Your steadfastness is beyond measure—your faithfulness to be treasured.

I come to you each morning, saying much the same thing over and over. Each day I want to tell you how much I love and honor you. Then I turn around and fail you so often.

Grow your fruit in me. (Galatians 5:22-23). And may I grow in trust so your fruit is seen by others and they find hope in you—all through your power, not mine. (Romans 15:13).

There is hurt, anger, and frustration at every turn. Bind Satan so there can be healing. It is in your name that I pray. Love, honor, and praise as I pray Joshua 24:15 for me and my family.

— *Day 25* —

Lord, today instead of starting with a praise and thanksgiving, I am asking for a growing trust and faith. I want to trust you with my whole being. When I focus on you and your presence with me, my trust grows. There are areas that I can trust you so easily; and then along comes a mountain or a chasm and I need complete concentration and a total commitment. Lord, grow me in you. (Psalm 23:4).

Thank you for your constant presence—even when I am not aware of it. Your Word with its promises is comforting and gives strength. I can look back and see you and all that you have done for me. Thank you.

I want to relax in your healing presence today—right now. Transform me through this time with you. (Romans 12:2). May I be a channel for your love to others—in your power, now mine. Help me walk in ways that please you, reflecting your healing love and light. (Ephesians 5:15-16).

I am asking, just as David asked, "Write your Word on my heart that I may not sin against you." I fail you so often, but "Your Word is a lamp to my feet and a light to my path." (Psalm 119:105).

As I walk close to you, may I saturate my mind with Your Word and allow you to show me how to spend my time and energy taking the "next right step."

You know my cares and concerns and I give them to you. My prayer is Joshua 24:15. Bind Satan from me and each of my family. Only you can do that.

Love, honor, praise and thanks!

— *Day 26* —

Lord, I am so thankful that you are with me all the time and for your special presence with me this morning. The King of kings—the Lord of lords—in my house—on my patio—with me—talking to me—WOW!

I want to know you better; I want to hear your voice and follow your guidance. Lord, "awaken my ear to listen like one being taught." (Isaiah 50:4). It is through you that I know how to function—and even then, I mess up. Help me, Lord.

I want to live close enough to you that I reflect your light—through your power, not mine. I want your love to flow through me to others giving hope; may they feel your kindness.

Thank you that I can come directly into your presence at any time. Thank you for tearing that temple curtain from top to bottom so that I am no longer separated from you and the Father. (Matthew 27:50-51). I can come to you any time I want to.

My prayer is Joshua 24:15 for me and each of my family. Fill us with your fruit. (Galatians 5:22-23). May I give kindness and encouragement to each person I meet today—overlooking no one.

I am yours. Even though I am nothing or a nobody of significance—the least in your kingdom—I love and honor you.

— *Day 27* —

Lord, thank you for all that you are: sovereign, holy, loving, and on and on and on! Your blessings are too numerous to list. When I think about your carrying my sins to the cross for me, I am "undone." You took my lashes and my nails and you shed your blood that I could live with you and the Father. Then you rose from the grave victorious! Then you sent the Holy Spirit—your Spirit—to live in me—to comfort and counsel me. Lord, I owe you everything.

Today, I want to relax in your everlasting arms (Deuteronomy 33:27) and grow in my awareness of your almighty presence. Lord, you are all I need; you are sufficient. You provide an abundance of blessing. I am asking that you grow your fruit in me.

As I age and my energy wanes, may I grow strong in you. Help me use all my energy trusting you. I want to go through this day leaning on you and allowing your love to flow through me. May the fruit you grow in me (love, peace, joy, patience, kindness, goodness, faithfulness, gentleness, and self-control) strengthen each of your children I encounter today.

May I use your strength and power today to bind Satan from me and my family so we are fully free to serve you. (Joshua 24:15). Lord, our nation needs you desperately.

Lord, I love, honor, and praise you.

— *Day 28* —

It may be same ole beginning; but, Lord, you have done and continue to do so much for me that I have to start with "Thank you" and that still is not enough.

Your love is beyond measure. (Ephesians 3:16-19). May my heart and mind be open to receive your love in full measure all the way to my core. Your love is unending, boundless, everlasting. It's unconditional—you love us all—the whole world! Help me learn to love others that same way. Today may I go with you gently, loving and encouraging each of your children as I walk fully aware of your presence.

Lord, as I spill out my wants and desires to you, let them be used to your glory. May everything I think, do, and say be to your glory. May my actions give a glimpse of who You are, your nature, your power, your loving kindness. I know you don't need me because the stars and all of heaven constantly reveal your glory better than I ever could. (Psalm 19:1). But I need you desperately!

And, Lord, I need you to make your glory known to me. Let my requests be opportunities for me to witness your glory firsthand. You are my Provider, Healer, (2 Kings 20:5), Sustainer, (Psalm 54:4), Wisdom (1Corinthians 1:25), Creator, Savior, Protector, Friend, Counselor.... my all.

Lord, may I always praise and honor you by giving thanks for all you do! May I always tell others what you have done—brag on you! May my life be to your glory. In your name I pray Joshua 24:15 for me and my family.

— Day 29 —

Thank you for another day, your presence, and your unfailing love. Your constancy is beyond my understanding; help me truly grasp that. (Jeremiah 31:3).

Today, I want to release my cares and concerns to you so that I might hear and know your voice. As everything changes around me, help me keep my eyes and awareness on you. You are the same, today, yesterday, and always. (Hebrews 13:8). May I draw strength from you, be a channel for your love to others, and glorify you in all that I do. My need for you is as constant as is your love for me.

Right now, I am in a privileged position in your kingdom, wearing this "robe of righteousness" that you bought for me with your blood. Help me walk close to you as I practice "being like you." (Isaiah 61:10). When my behavior isn't fit for your kingdom, help me get rid of—throw off—that behavior. (Ephesians 4:22-24).

At this moment, I am enjoying the beautiful outdoors you created, my coffee, and your presence. Thank you, Lord. I love and praise you.

My motto for today is Trust! Thank! and Live lightheartedly.

— *Day 30* —

Lord, may my mind and heart be open to sense and appreciate the full measure of your love and the price you paid for me to able to come directly into your presence. I do believe your love for me is boundless and that you are with me now. Your Spirit lives within me.

You are with me and all around me. I am surrounded by your Light. You can see me because you are infinite; nothing escapes your notice. You love each and every one of your children; and yet, you love me as if it were just the two of us—you and me in this world.

You are my closest, dearest friend, still you are the Creator of the universe and my sovereign Lord. You have the supreme power to establish anything or destroy everything and yet you are gentle enough to wipe away my tears.

I do have the ability to know you as Friend and Lord at the same time— but I want to know you more and more each day. Yes, I am "fearlessly and wonderfully made." (Psalm 139:14). Thank you for making me capable of receiving and responding to your presence.

Give me strength so I am not "conformed to the patterns of this world, but transformed by the renewing of my mind." (Romans 12:2). Lord, bind Satan from me and grow your fruit in me. (James 4:7-8 and Galatians 5:22-23). Today show me the person(s) you want to touch through me; may I encourage and love according to your plan.

Love, praise, and honor go to you.

— *Day 31* —

I am truly blessed! Thank you for all your blessings, but especially for this time in your intimate presence. Help me be aware of your continual presence—only you can provide that comfort. And, since you created me, you know my heart, my mind, my spirit. The amazing part is that you still love me. And to top it off, you clothed me in a robe of righteousness when I called on your name. (Luke 12:7; John 1:12 ; Romans 10:13).

What a love story! You love my soul, understand me perfectly, and will love me right on into heaven and forever.

May my thoughts and my ways become more and more like yours. I want to reflect you and your love in every contact I have. I want to live in union with you. I want the fulfillment that comes from yielding to you—living close to you. In that, I am complete and can bless others through your power.

Lord, never let me use the freedom I have found in you to be used selfishly, arrogantly, or deliberately insensitive to any one; may the knowledge I have of the freedom there is in you be used to build others up in love.

Forgive me because I have sinned against you and I am truly sorry. I lay my cares and concerns down at your feet. I love you, Lord, and praise you as I pray Joshua 24:15.

Today
With You

— *Day 1* —

Lord, thank you for this morning and this time with you. Even though my thoughts are not your thoughts and my ways are not your ways, (Isaiah 55:8-9), I want them to be. I want to be like you. I want to know you more intimately. Anyone who would go to the cross for me, I want to know all there is to know about him.

Today, help me trust you with all my thoughts. Help me direct all my thoughts toward you and through your love. Remind me to practice trust and thanksgiving. I want to reject each negative and sinful thought, confessing each one to you and then leave them at the foot of the cross. You are "faithful and just and will forgive me my sins if I confess them to you." (1 John 1:9). You alone can purify me from all unrighteousness. I am asking you to sanctify me through and through. (1 Thessalonians 5:23). I want to stay aware of your presence with me.

You told Satan to leave you alone—stop tempting you—and he did! (Matthew 4:10-11). I want him to leave me and my family alone. I want to use your power for that also. I want to leave Satan powerless and defeated so we are free to serve and glorify you.

Jesus, Lord and Savior, I am asking you to send your angels to protect each of my family and continue to hold them close to you.

This day is yours, Lord. All honor, praise, and love belong to you.

— *Day 2* —

Lord, regardless of all else, I have to thank you for allowing this special time in God's presence—through you. You made it all possible and it cost you so much. Thank you for this privilege. Thank you for the joy and comfort it brings. Help me continue throughout the day meditating on your Word, thinking about your laws and how to best follow them as I go about my day. I would like to feel all day the same closeness with you that I feel now.

Thank you for the joy you give as I trust in you. (Psalm 2:12b).

Lord, you who gives patience, steadiness, and encouragement, help me live in harmony with others. May I have your attitude. (Romans 15:5). May I be a channel of love and encouragement to each person I meet today. I want to be a voice for you, glorifying you and the Father. (Romans 15:6).

May I grow deeper in you. May my roots be deep in you so I will be steadfast and firm—so the storms of life will not move me. (I don't know the words I want to use; but, Lord, you know my heart. Purify it. Sanctify me.)

Bind Satan from me and each of my family. I am asking for your whole army of protective angels if that's what is necessary to put a hedge around us.

I love, praise, and honor you; and I am praying Joshua 24:15.

— *Day 3* —

Lord, I never want to take for granted your intimate presence with me. Help me marvel each morning at the wonder of your continual nearness. And, the thing I marvel at most is: you know everything about me and yet you still love me and want me to spend time with you. You knew all about me before you went to the cross and you still went! That's one of the greatest wonders in my world!

Lord, I want to learn to give thanks to you for all things (Ephesians 5:20)—even when all seems to be going wrong. Help me trust you because your Word is true. (Romans 8:28). Remind me to call on your name, affirming my trust and giving thanks. Your promise never to leave me assures me you will see me through—each step of the way. Let me be like Habakkuk. (3:17-19).

May I be clothed in strength and dignity and have the ability to laugh at the days to come. (Proverbs 31:25). May I have a cheerful heart and allow your love, peace, and joy flow through me to each of those around me. (Proverbs 17:22).

Thank you for letting me leave my cares and concerns with you. I'm asking you to bind Satan from me and my family. I am also lifting up our nation's, state's, cities', churches', families' leaders to you for guidance and courage to follow you.

I love, praise, and honor you.

— *Day 4* —

Lord, you are the Creator of heaven and earth—Lord of all! Then you amaze me by choosing to live within me. Fill me, Lord, with your love, joy, and peace—permeate me with your presence. You are infinite and yet you choose to be my helper. (John 14:16-17).

So often, Lord, when a situation seems like a "no-brainer", I "go it alone." That's when I really mess up. Forgive me and help me remember to come to you first, asking for your guidance and strength. I need you each step of the way...small step or large step. Without you, my glorious Source of Strength, I am nothing. It is you who lifts me out of and above my circumstances. I can only offer thanks and gratitude. (Ephesians 5:20).

Lord, I want my trust in you to grow. I want to be able to honestly say—all the time—"But I trust in your unfailing love, my heart rejoices in your salvation." (Psalm 13:5).

May I humble myself under your mighty hand and give you all my anxieties and cares. (1 Peter 5:6-7). It is in you that I find peace. This day may I be a living sacrifice to you as my act of worship. I want you to transform me by renewing my mind so that I walk with you, according to your good, pleasing, and perfect will. (Romans 12:1-2).

Joshua 24:15 remains my prayer—with love, honor, and praise.

— *Day 5* —

Lord, today I want to make everything around me secondary to living close to you and finding the joy that comes from being in your presence. I want to be able to say Habakkuk 3:17-19 and mean every word.

I repeat "you are God of the universe—Creator of it all" and you just revealed to me more evidence about your character. You care about every little detail in my life—you've said it often times in your Word to me. In Exodus 26:1-5 the message is "I care about every detail even down to the number of loops I want on this curtain that is to be hung in the temple where I reside." (I am the temple where you reside now.) **Wow!** Lord, I didn't get that said very well, but I had to get that much down on paper so that I don't forget your message to me this morning.

You are the Creator—yet you are here with me! You are the Creator— yet every detail about your temple where you reside is to be just so. You don't explain why you want it exactly that way except to say "become a single unit." (10 sheets a certain length and a certain width, and certain colors, hung a certain way.) Lord, this morning help me learn how to build on this temple (me) according to your specifications.

Bind Satan from me and my family so we may be a glory to you. Joshua 24:15 is my prayer.

I love, honor, praise you and ask for clear, specific guidance.

— *Day 6* —

Lord, this time with you is so precious and so is the time in your Word. Just being in your presence brings peace; then I open your Word and find all these wonderful love notes you have for me. "I will not forget you. I have inscribed you on the palms of my hands." (Isaiah 49:15-16). Thank you.

Lord, help me see and remember all you have done for me. (Deuteronomy 4:9 & 8:11). Joshua built a memorial in the middle of the river (Joshua 4) to be a reminder of you. The Lord's Supper is a reminder of your sacrifice for us. (Luke 22:19).

I never want to forget your goodness, your steadfastness, your sovereignty, your presence, your unconditional sacrificial love. As I remember all this as well as your promises, my trust and faith find fertile ground in which to grow. May this also open my eyes and alert me to see you and your blessings I might have missed otherwise.

Lord, give me a willingness to follow wherever you lead. You know what lies ahead and let that be enough for me. You have never failed me. Help me learn to live by faith—(2 Corinthians) remembering what I have seen.

Bind Satan from me and each of my family that we may serve you. (Joshua 24:15.) My love, honor, praise, and thanksgiving belong to you.

— *Day 7* —

Lord, this day is yours, and I want to spend it with you. I love this quiet time with you; let me take this awareness of you with me throughout the day. You are always present—I want to learn or develop a constant awareness of that truth. You are omnipresent!

Help me be vigilant against the schemes of the devil. You are with me, but he doesn't give up. He is out roaming around planning ways to draw me away from you. (1 Peter 5:8). You are victorious; but he knows my weaknesses, and he will tempt me trying to lure me away. You will hold me; I don't want anything to come between us. I want you to be first in my life. Thank you for your Word. Thank you for your whole armor. (Ephesians 6:10-18). Help me put it on.

Lord, I am bringing you my worries and my every care, and I am placing them in your everlasting arms. I want to remember this whole day that you are in charge of all that—so I can seek your face wholeheartedly. I want to be so open that you can soak into me—all the way into every crevice of my being.

Whatever this day holds, help me accept it as a part of your plan. Then, Lord, help me learn quickly what you want me to learn from it and be what you want me to be in it. (Psalm 118:24).

Infidelity is a sin; so is complaining. Let me not condemn the one while committing the other. I just want to be yours, trusting you, praising who you are, giving thanks for all my blessings.

Bind Satan from me and each of my family. Send your angels to protect and provide a hedge. Thank you. Love. Honor. Praise. (Joshua 24:15).

— *Day 8* —

Lord, your unconditional, constant love continues to be beyond my ability to grasp—much less copy. I want to learn and grow to be like you, but I can't do that if I don't learn to love like you love. Your love never fails. (Hebrews 13:8). You have redeemed me; you guide, lead, and strengthen me. Help me follow close to you. (Exodus 15:13). Draw me to you with loving kindness. (Jeremiah 31:3).

You never promised a life of ease, but I continue to ask for it. Forgive me. Strengthen me to "take up my cross daily" in ways that will glorify you. (Luke 9:23). I am nothing and can do nothing without you— and I am fearful. You know all about my weaknesses; help me learn to depend on you to supply all my needs. I want to walk by faith; I can only hope I am not too old to learn to do that. By myself I am inadequate to cope with the changes that are happening so rapidly. I trust you with eternity; teach me to trust you with tomorrow, and today as well.

Thank you for who you are—the God/Man who went to the cross for me. Thank you for sending your Spirit to counsel and comfort me each step I take. Thank you, God/Father for everything—especially revealing yourself through your Son. Thank you for the unity of you three—Father, Son, and Spirit.

Bind Satan from me and my family so there is glory to you. Love, honor, praise belong to you.

— *Day 9* —

Lord, this crisp fall morning is just one of your blessings; the greatest blessings are your resurrection and your constant, faithful, loving presence. May I give thanks to you in all circumstances. (1 Thessalonians 5:18).

Thank you for allowing me to bring my cares and concerns to you—even the same ones that I thought I had left with you yesterday, last week, even last month. You know my weakness of wanting things my way. Forgive me and help me see every situation from your perspective. Thank you for letting me stay close to you until I see "it" your way.

Lord, close my mouth—seal my lips—until I do see "it" your way. I don't want to gripe or complain against you and your permissive will. Let me continue to tell you what I want, but never let it be a complaint. (Philippians 4:14-15). Just put your thoughts in my mind and your song in my heart.

Lord, grow my trust in you—until I **know** you are with me—that I am never separated from you. May everything—everything—teach me; grow me until I trust you totally (Genesis 50:20) and become the person you want me to be.

May I not be conformed to the patterns of this world. (Romans 12:2). May I be transformed by renewing my mind with whatever is honorable, just, pure, lovely, YOU. (Philippians 4:8).

Bind Satan from me and my family so that we may boldly serve you. All honor, praise, and love go to you.

— *Day 10* —

Thank you, Lord, for your presence with me now; help me love you with all my heart, soul, strength, and mind—and my neighbor as myself. (Luke 10:27). May everything I do be done in a way that pleases and glorifies you. You paid dearly on the cross for me—and my body is your temple. Help me use it for your glory. (1 Corinthians 10:31; 1 Peter 4:11). May you be my first priority.

And, Lord, as I make you my first priority—help me learn to trust you enough to let things happen without trying to predict or control them. I want to learn to relax and refresh myself in your loving presence.

Instead of fearing my weaknesses and inadequacies, I want to trust and rejoice in your abundant supply. (Psalm 37:3-6). Even when I think I can handle a situation by myself, help me train my mind to bring all things (everything) to you first—even the daily, trivial, mundane things.

Lord, show me areas I need to bring to you in repentance—show me specifically so I can commit them to you before I reach the throne of judgment.

Bind Satan from me and my family. (Joshua 24:15). May each one of us grow in awe and reverence of you. Lord, you know I love, honor, and praise you even as I often fail you.

— *Day 11* —

Lord, thank you for the multitude of blessings you have brought into my life—but most of all, I thank you for your constant presence. With Satan roaming all around me, it is your presence that shields and protects me. Thank you. Every good and perfect gift comes from you. (James 1:17).

Lord, reveal each of my flaws to me that I can bring them to you. I want to be honest with myself and with you. "You know my folly, O God; my guilt is not hidden from you." (Psalm 69:5) and may I never judge someone else. (Matthew 7:1-2). I want to be ever-mindful of the grace you have given me—the grace I continue to need each day. Take away any pride I have; and let me breathe in your grace so I can show your love to each person I meet today. Lord, in you alone, "I can clothe myself with humility toward others. You resist the proud and give grace to the humble." (1 Peter 5:5).

Lord, may I become transparent, loving, helpful, obedient! And, today, I want to take the next right step to become that. I am giving you my cares and concerns. I am yours; my cares and concerns are yours too! Thank you for all that you are doing as you answer my prayers.

Bind Satan from me and my family—each one. Joshua 24:15 is my prayer today. I love, honor, and praise you.

— *Day 12* —

Lord, you are gracious and so lovingly kind to me. Nothing I am or nothing I could do would deserve your love and care. Thank you. You are here with me now; I want to continue this awareness of your presence throughout the day.

I know "without faith it is impossible to please you." (Hebrews 11:6). May my faith grow as I spend time with you and seek your guidance. I want to become more and more honest with you.

I know you love me; you proved it; you died for me. I know you are omnipresent—always with me. Help me see myself from your standard. You are omniscient—all knowing. Your gaze is steady and sure. From the cross, you looked down on me with loving, forgiving eyes. May I rest peacefully as I look back at you: worshiping you, praising you, honoring you. May I worship you in spirit and truth (John 4:23-24) and lay my sins at the foot of the cross.

Lord, I am so concerned about my grandchildren—the decisions they are making and the lives they are choosing for themselves. I have to remember you love them and care about them, even more than I do. They are in a world where your Word is flaunted and defiled. Satan is "roaming, looking to destroy them." Guide and protect them, Lord.

Never let me interfere with your plan for them. Close my mouth until I can say the words you want me to say. Then give me courage and grace to say **exactly** what you want me to say in the way you want it said— with love. Until then, Lord, send your army of angels to protect us all.

Bind Satan this day—in your power, not mine. I am yours. My family is yours. May we serve you and be a glory to you. (Joshua 24:15).

— *Day 13* —

Lord, as I come to you this morning thanking you for your presence with me and this time alone with you, I repeat things I have said to you before more than once. I love, honor, and praise you. Forgive me of my sin(s) and reveal to me the sin(s) I do not see. Grow my faith and trust in you. Help me release my idea that I have control over anything. Help me submit to you. Grow your fruit in me that I may be a blessing to others that I encounter along the way. Protect my family and me. Bind Satan. May I (we) always be faithful to serve and glorify your name. Yes, Lord, I say it over and over.

Well, Lord, I do love, honor, and praise you as I have in the past. I do want to be more pleasing to you today than I was yesterday. My behaviors yesterday—my thoughts—were not all as they should have been; forgive me. Is my faith and trust in you stronger today than it was yesterday? I hope that they are, but I'm not certain they are. And, on and on. Lord, I want to be honest with you and with myself.

You are God! You know all things as they are! I don't want to try to hide things from you and "kinda" wash over them. Help me be real and authentic with you.

Hold my hand, Lord, as we walk through this day together. You have the power to bind Satan; and when I am in your presence, I am protected. May my family—each one—find that same protection. (Joshua 24:15).

This day is yours. (Psalm 46:10). Help me "Be still and know that you are God!"

— *Day 14* —

Lord, thank you for this day and this time with you. Yes, Lord, I fail you often and I am again asking your forgiveness. Redeem me from my sin ("mistakes" wouldn't be the right word—not strong enough). May I become more humble and grace-filled when I recognize your grace, your wisdom, and the correction you have for me.

I have asked that you grow me in faith and trust. I should know "growth" is most often found in pain and difficulty. May I see them as opportunities to demonstrate the trust I do have, give you thanks and praise, and grow. I know you are sovereign and can bring good out of everything. (Romans 8:28). I want to be mature and complete; forgive me for wanting faith and trust without doing my part. (James 1:2-4).

May I give thanks for your unfailing love and wonderful acts of mercy to me. May I tell of your grace, mercy, and faithfulness with joy. (Psalm 107:21-22).

I beg, pray, plead, beseech you that I and each of my family will walk in intense love for you, reverently fearing your holy name and loving our neighbors as ourselves. I am blessed because I believe in you as the Son of God who came to shed your blood for my sin. I do trust you, rely on you. My hope and confidence is in you. (Jeremiah 17:7).

Bind Satan from me, Lord. My love, honor, and praise are due you.

— *Day 15* —

Lord, somehow I got interrupted before I spent time with you this morning. When I come to you and am fully aware of your presence, you provide all sorts of blessings. I don't want to miss any one of them! I want to enjoy all the blessings you provide for me just by my coming and being fully aware of your presence. (Matthew 28:20).

I want to be conscious of you with every step I take. Your promise to be with me to the very end of the age is a promise that strengthens me and gives me courage. When I am aware of your presence, staying close to you, I can avoid many of the snares that would trap me if you weren't there guiding me.

When I take my eyes off you, I can slip into pride and self-will. Or, I can just as easily go to the pit of self-pity, despair, and resentment. Lord, I need your protection. I want nothing/no one to take your place with me.

Lord, help me get rid of everything that interferes with my relationship to you. May I faithfully persevere each day on the path you have set for me, and may I do that with joy that gives hope to others—not in my power, but yours. (Hebrews 12:1-2 and Romans 15:13).

I am really wanting to "get my mind around" thanking you for my problems and trials. All I can do at this moment is thank you for being with me at this stage of my life and know you are working things out for my good. (Romans 8:28).

Joshua 24:15 is my prayer and I need you to bind Satan from me and my family if we are to be a glory to you. You have my love, praise, and thanksgiving.

— *Day 16* —

Lord, I'm not sure what was the first thing that interfered with my time with you. After the first thing interfered, I allowed another and another thing to interfere until I had a whole series of things and now it is bedtime. I don't want a whole day to pass when I have not had time alone with you. I need you! Today is Sunday and I have had SS, church, small group and a gospel concert, but what I need most is you and you alone.

Even though it's late, I am turning my thoughts to you. And though I am speaking to you, I really want to hear your voice. I want your active presence in all that I do. When I am aware of you, it's easier for me to find peace and joy. It's easier to quiet the anxieties. You tell me not to worry. (Luke 12:22-26).

Lord, may I quietly rest in the assurance of your constant presence, knowing you are in control. Help me joyfully submit to your leadership and learn to see every situation from your perspective.

You are the God of hope; fill me with joy and peace as I trust you so that I may overflow with hope by your power—not mine. (Romans 15:13).

You can do more than I can even imagine much less ask for. (Ephesians 3:20). I am asking you to continue to bind Satan from me and my family so we may serve you faithfully. (Joshua 24:15).

Love and praise go to you.

— *Day 17* —

Lord, thank you for being you, Lover of my soul. Thank you for allowing me to look to you where I can find help, comfort, and companionship, as well as strength. (Psalm 105:4). You are always with me whether I am walking Aries or sitting here in the early morning specifically talking with you. Even the briefest glance can connect me to you because you are always here with me.

When I come to you for help or guidance, you allow it to flow freely to me—in large matters or the smallest one. Knowing I need you keeps me spiritually alive. I am seeking your face.

When I come to you for comfort, you tenderly wrap me in your loving arms so I feel comforted. You meet my needs and sustain me. You are at the same time teaching me to comfort others; I am doubly blessed. (2 Corinthians 1:3-4).

Just knowing you never leave me—you are always there—is one of the greatest blessings I find in the salvation you bought for me on the cross. Your constant companionship is the "Cream of the Crop." (Sorry, Lord, to sound so earthy, but then you know me.) Without you, I am nothing!

This day is yours and I am leaving my cares and concerns with you. I continue to pray Joshua 24:15 and ask you to guard each of my family from harmful relationships so that we might glorify you.

I love you, praise you, honor you and give you thanks.

— *Day 18* —

Thank you again, Lord, for being God as you are—Son of God, the Father. Yes, thank you for the abundant life you brought with you (John 10:10) and for the hope of life eternal in you. And, thank you for this moment right now in your presence.

Lord, as old as I am and with all the times I have seen how faithful you are, you would think I would automatically trust you when trials appear. On my knees, I humbly ask you to grow my faith and teach me to trust you as I take the next step. I want to be obedient and open to your guidance. I want to make the right choices—ones that reflect your love.

Lord, it's about time that we as a nation switch back to CST (Central Standard Time) from Daylight Savings Time. CST and DST are not important. I just want to learn GPT (God's Perfect Time). When I give you a situation to solve, I want you to take care of it immediately. Yes, you are taking care of it, but on GPT. Help me give thanks as I learn to tell GPT. Also, Lord, keep me from being a stumbling block as you "work things out for my good" on your time. (Romans 8:28).

You are omniscient; you know my concerns. You are omnipotent; you can handle them all. You are omnipresent; I thank you, praise you, and love you for being with me. (Joshua 24:15).

— *Day 18 again* —

Lord, you know last night was not a typical night. I thought it was 6:00 a.m. when in reality it was only midnight. The best part of it all is you were as ready to spend time with me then as you are right now. That is just one of the things I love about you; you are always ready to spend time with me.

Lord, I can come to you for understanding, since you know me better than I know myself. Nothing about me is hidden from you. "You have searched me and you know me...when I sit, when I rise, what my thoughts are, what my words will be." (Psalm 139:1-4). After all that, the amazing part is you still love me.

May the light of your healing presence shine into the deepest parts of me—cleansing me, healing me, refreshing me, and renewing me. I want to learn to trust you completely. Lord, am I asking you for understanding or discernment? (Of course, you know I need both.)

You have put your seal of ownership on me (2 Corinthians 1:21-22). I want to trust your guarantee for "today and tomorrow" with the same certainty as I trust you for eternity. (Joshua 1:5).

May I simply draw closer and closer to you, rejoicing that you do understand me, will give me the discernment I need, and love me perfectly. Lord, fill me with your love until it overflows to others.

Joshua 24:15 is still my prayer as I love, praise, honor you....giving thanks.

— *Day 19* —

Lord, I am here with my defenses down. May I be open and authentic with you; nothing is hidden from you! May I allow your Word to expose my thoughts and intentions, encourage, and transform me. That's the reason you went to the cross—you knew all about me and knew I needed a Savior. That's the reason you sent your Spirit to live within me. You knew I would need all that you could do for me. (Exodus 33:14).

Lord, I just want to "practice" being in your presence, communing with you, worshiping you, glorifying you. It is only in you that I am able to smile with your joy and love others with your love. (1 John 1:5-7).

Thank you for your Word: your Love Letter to me, your Instruction Manual! It is alive and exactly what I need. (Hebrews 4:12). Even small nuggets show me new ways to live in you—with you. I ask for more insight as all of it is relevant and true to my daily reality—no matter where I am or what I am doing. It is alive, active, and sharp with power to get to my innermost thoughts. Lord, you are the Word. (John 1:1).

As I think about the Scriptures (ponder your Word), Lord, allow them to enter my mind, to make their way to my heart, to open up space for you to have your way with me.

May your Word teach me how to seek, understand, enjoy you as well as give me discernment. Let it absorb deeply within me, exposing my thoughts and intentions, encouraging and transforming me. May it come alive to me, in me, and through me.

I am yours and my prayer continues to be Joshua 24:15. Love, honor, and praise to you.

— *Day 20* —

Lord, I am yours and I seek your face again this morning. And, again I come with my defenses down, asking you to reveal my sins to me that I do not see; also asking your help in confessing them to you as if you didn't know all about them already. I don't want there to be any barriers between us. It's not possible, Lord, but I would like to "walk in the garden" with you as Adam and Eve first did. Until I get to heaven, this TAG on the patio will have to do.

May my focus this day be communion with you; may everything I do and say today be worship and glory to you.

Thank you for who you are: God, Creator, Sustainer, Savior, and on and on! May I learn to identify more and more with you. I want my life to become more and more intertwined with you—growing stronger each day. May I live so close to you that I become more alive spiritually even as my body ages.

May your life shine through me as I walk in your light. (1 John 1:7). And, I want my thoughts to be noble, right, pure, lovely, and admirable. (Philippians 4:8).

My prayer continues to be Joshua 24:15, and I continue to ask for your power to bind Satan from me and my family.

— *Day 21* —

Lord, I come this morning asking for your help—help in submitting to you. I say I want to submit, but somehow I resist doing that in reality. I want to live contently in your presence; that I am certain of. Yet, when something interferes with "my" plans, I can be resentful, wanting things my way—now!

Let me start over by giving thanks to you for all things: salvation, family, friends, health, abilities, possessions. These are all gifts from you. (Job 1:21). When I begin to act and feel as though I am entitled to these gifts, remind me they were your gifts to me—I didn't deserve any of them. May I learn gratitude. Let me learn to love all your gifts freely, but love you more. (Psalm 139:23-24).

I say I love your sovereignty and I do; it gives order to this world. But, when your sovereignty interferes with "my" world, I often complain and become resentful. Forgive me and help me learn to give thanks and humble myself under your mighty hand. (1 Peter 5:6).

It is uncomfortable realizing some very ugly things about myself; but with exposure, I can allow you to renew and refresh me in the truth of your Word. It is only in you that I have value, peace, and joy. I want to be more like you.

My prayer is again Joshua 24:15. You deserve my love, praise, honor, and especially my thanks and gratitude.

— *Day 22* —

Lord, I am so grateful that I can come to you wearing the "robe of righteousness" you bought for me with your blood. Otherwise, I would be hiding in shame just as Adam and Eve did when they realized their sin. Shame is powerful, but isn't it just the surface of fear?

The fear may be fear of not getting what I want, fear of being rejected, fear that others won't value me, fear of being seen as I really am. Lord, you know everything about me; everything about me is bare and wide open to your all-seeing eyes. (Hebrews 4:13). Still you loved me and died for me.

As I live in you—in your perfect love—I pray my love will become more like yours. In you, I will not be ashamed and embarrassed; but I can come to you with confidence asking forgiveness because you do love me. (1 John 4:17-18).

Satan continues to try to steal my joy, weaken my witness, kill my motivation by continually reminding me of my guilt and shame. I must remember Satan is a liar. I must also remember that on the cross you demonstrated your love for me once and for all. And after three days in the grave, you rose victorious. I have nothing left to fear and my shame is covered.

You have all power to keep every one of your wonderful promises. Thank you! Thank you! Thank you! All love, honor, and praise belong to you. Joshua 24:15 continues to be my commitment.

— *Day 23* —

Hallelujah! Yes, praise you! How good it is to sing your praises! How delightful and how right! (Psalm 147:1). Thank you for being right here with me. I don't have to shout; you can hear me when I whisper your praises. You know all my thoughts even as I think them and before I think them. You are omniscient; yes, hallelujah! You are omnipresent, hallelujah! You are omnipotent, hallelujah! Thank you for being you and for loving me.

Lord, my praises to you were interrupted earlier. I am so glad it came at a time when I would be remembering how much you love us and how magnificent you are. May that love flow through me to others.

Truly, you are the victorious King of kings and Lord of lords—the sovereign Creator—the Son of God who loved me enough to die on the cross and descend into hell for me. Thank you, Lord. You have more than earned my love and devotion. May your Spirit give me strength and courage to live in ways that glorify you and show just how much I love you.

You know my weaknesses, Lord, and each one amplifies my need for you. As I depend on you more and more, may others see you at work in me. Lord, I don't want to follow just any path; help me walk close to you and leave a definite trail for others to follow. Guide me in paths of righteousness for your name's sake. (Psalm 23:3). Guide my feet into the path of peace so those who are living in darkness can see the trail leading to you. (Luke1:79). You have shown me the path of life and you continue to fill me with the joy your presence brings. (Acts 2:28). Lord, fill me to overflowing with your fruit as I trust you so that others may find hope. (Romans 15:13).

You are already doing immeasurably more for me than I can imagine or ask for so I am leaving my cares and concerns in your hands. (Ephesians 3:20). When I simply say Joshua 24:15, you know all that connects to it. Thank you. My love, praise, and honor go to you.

— *Day 24* —

Lord, you are my light and my salvation—whom should I fear? You are the stronghold of my life—of whom should I be afraid? (Psalm 27:1). David was running for his life, hiding in caves, dodging swords at the dinner table and he could still sense and know your presence. Lord, I want that kind of awareness.

Peter who was hanged tells me to give you all my worries and care. He knew that you are always thinking about each of us and are watching over us. (1 Peter 5:7). And you yourself—the Son of God who was crucified—tell me to give no thought for tomorrow. (Matthew 6:25-26).

You are God with me, for all time and throughout eternity. I don't want the awareness of your presence to grow dull and lose its impact. My cares and concerns are nothing in comparison to any of the early day Christians—and you sustained them. And I know you will sustain me 'cause you promised never to leave me. You are faithful to keep your promises. I want your constant presence to be a continual source of joy, springing up and flowing out to others.

Even in my busiest moments, I want to remain conscious of your presence so that with each encounter I can touch others through you power. Today—all day long—I want to tell you about the things that delight me as well as the things that distress me. May I do that every day as I keep close to you.

Lord, you are with me; I want to grow in you, trusting you more and more each day. Joshua 24:15 is my prayer and all love, praise, and honor belong to you.

— *Day 25* —

Lord, forgive me when I start a day without coming to you first, and leave you sitting there waiting for me to join you. I just need to start this day aware of your presence, your love, your grace. I am yours and want to remember this day with you.

Lord, you are so magnificent—so creative. Your lessons come so often in unexpected ways—not always to be read, memorized, written, talked, etc. Your Word is the basis of instruction and it tells me how I am to relate to you and others. As your slave, I must not quarrel, I am to be gentle, able to teach, patient and instructing opponents with gentleness." (2 Timothy 2:24-25).

You are sovereign and in it all. Each person I meet is there by your permission or design—those I click with, even those that irritate me to the "inth degree." Maybe especially those! They may not know you or maybe they are new in you. They may need to see "You" in "me." I need to rely on you and your Word for guidance. Whoever they are, whatever their views or biases, may my response be one that glorifies you.

Lord, may I always ask for your wisdom and rely on your grace... because how often do I quarrel with you about what I want? how often do I irritate you to the "inth degree"? how often do I demand my own way?

Thank you for each person you put in my path—even the irritating ones. If I am going to learn the lessons you are teaching, I must practice, practice, practice, practice. And, though my learning to deal with people may lead to more harmony, the end result is not for my peace—but for your glory.

May I learn to give "them" the same grace you gave and continue to give me. Lord, I need you. You are in all circumstances—each one. And, I need you to keep me humble, gentle, and usable if I am to be a part of your plan.

I pray Joshua 24:15. Hold me and each of my family close to you.

— *Day 26* —

Lord, thank you for your Word that reassures me of your love.

Yes, I know you died on the cross for me and then rose again. Yes, you meet me every morning and are with me constantly. But, your Word gives another beautiful—even vivid—picture of how much you love me. As my groom, I am your bride; and as my groom, you rejoice over me as I walk down the aisle toward you. (Isaiah 62:5).

Regardless of how inadequate I feel, how many times I fail you, I must never underestimate your love for me. You call me by different names: "my delight is in her, Redeemed, Cared for." (Isaiah 62). You are not apathetic toward me; you view me "with fierce affection". I am your "sought-after bride."

Wow! How can this day be anything but wonderful! You are my joyfully committed groom who will guide, guard, and keep care of me.

Help me remember all of this as I meet the world today. Let that security be so real that I can be the channel for your love to flow through to others.

Lord, thank you for allowing me to linger in your presence just a little longer this a.m., as you bathe me in your love. It equips me for the day ahead. Only you know what will happen today and I can rest in the security you give. In you, I "will not grow weary and lose heart." (Hebrews 12:3).

Again, Joshua 24:15 is my prayer. Hold me and each of my family close to you that we may be a glory to you. Bind Satan from each of us. Love, Praise, and Honor go to you, Lord.

— *Day 27* —

Lord, today, help me be attentive at all times to see your children through your eyes of love. You know I love you and love this quiet time with you; help me love your children and take time to give them the loving attention you want for them. You are so gracious and generous with me, Lord; help me be gracious with each one of yours. I know you hear me when I come asking for help and guidance. (Jeremiah 29:12-13).

Lord, you are the Good Shepherd and I am your sheep. I want to know you more perfectly, to recognize your voice, and to follow you. You gave me life and you protect me. No one can take me away from you. (John 10:14, 27-28). Even though Satan taunts me and tries to destroy me and my relationship with you, you are almighty, omnipotent, and victorious. You will never let that happen.

You have shown me what is good and how to draw close to you. Lord, I want to act justly with love and mercy and to walk humbly with you day after day. (Micah 6:8).

My decision again this day is to serve you—me and my household. (Joshua 24:15). Lord, give me strength and courage to follow through on that decision. Love, Honor, and Praise are due you.

— *Day 28* —

Lord, I am still the same weak, inadequate person I've always been, and I still come to you asking for your love, strength, and courage to do what you guide me to do. I want to follow you and not run ahead of you. And, I am so thankful you meet with me each morning as I seek your will for the day, ask forgiveness where I have already failed you, and leave my cares and concerns at your feet.

Thank you! You are beyond all expectations! (Ephesians 3:20). You are incomparable, indescribable, infallible, infinite, immutable, and on and on. Thank you! Thank you for caring about me!

Lord, you know my heart today (Luke 8:17); may it be attuned to you. I want to listen to you even as I listen to your other children. As one of them opens up to share his/her soul with me, I know I am on holy ground and need your guidance to respond appropriately. (Exodus 3:5). I want to think through you, live through you, and love through you. I am not my own. (1 Corinthians 6:19). Use me, Lord. You are alive within me.

Empower my listening as well as my speaking so that the **streams of living water** flow through me. (John 7:38). Let me be a channel of all your blessings: love, joy, peace, patience, kindness, goodness, faithfulness, gentleness, and self control. (Galatians 5:22-23).

And, Lord, you know I cannot pray Joshua 24:15 without lifting each of my family (house) up to you for your care, guidance, and protection. Love, Honor, and Praise all belong to you.

— *Day 29* —

Oh, what a beautiful day and you made it! And you are here with me in it! What a wonderful God you are...Father of my Lord Jesus Christ, the source of every mercy, and the one who so wonderfully comforts and strengthens me at every turn. (2 Corinthians 1:3-4).

Lord, I often thank you for your presence with me—maybe not often enough, but more often than I thank you for your omniscience. Today I particularly want to thank you for that.

I am always in need of your guidance—from the one who is all knowing. Help me keep my eyes on you and my ears listening for your voice. Help me be open and teachable.

You know the obstacles that are ahead. You may have planned them so I would lean on you, knowing I couldn't handle them alone. You desire that I grow stronger in you. Help me trust you more. Increase my faith that I may face each day knowing you are with me.

Lord, bathe me in your love and light that I might grow strong and be available to help others—through you. Make me a channel of blessing. May love, peace, joy, patience, kindness, goodness, faithfulness, gentleness, and self-control (Galatians 5:22-23) be in me for your use.

Help me submit to you and resist the devil (James 4:7) wherever I am.

Yes, you are sovereign and compassionate so I am leaving my cares with you. I love you, Lord.

— *Day 30* —

Thank you for your loving kindness, your daily provisions, and your ultimate sacrifice that I might live with you forever. And, now, thank you for being here with me.

Again, in these "wee" hours, help me do as David said (Psalm 23:1-3): lie down in green pastures, rest beside still waters, and allow you to restore my soul. Help me to follow your lead and glorify your name with each of life's changes. I am in your presence; help me unwind and seek your direction. Only here can I find peace and security.

I am yours; help me walk in ways that will be an example for others who desire to live in your peaceful presence. Right now, make me a channel of blessing for those around me who are hurting.

I am weak and have failed you so often. Forgive me. I need you. I want to trust you more each day. Today is yours. And, I am praying Joshua 24:15 and loving you.

— *Day 31* —

Again, thank you for all that you are: the Alpha and the Omega, Builder, Creator, Christ, Counselor, Comforter, Father, Friend, God, Guide, Healer, Help, Immanuel, Jehovah, Jesus, Judge, King of kings, Lord of lords, Messiah, Master, omnipotent, omniscient, omnipresent, Prince of Peace, Redeemer, Savior, Son, Spirit, Trinity, Teacher, the Vine, Word, Wisdom, Warrior, Yahweh. And then there is Architect, Author, Artist, Beginning and End, Deliverer, Defender, First and Last, Foundation, Fortress, Lion and Lamb, Love, Light, Lamp, Protector, Provider, Rock, Refuge, Shepherd, Shield, Sustainer, Truth, Universal.

And that is less than the tip of the iceberg. You are indescribable! There just aren't enough words. Thank you for all you have done for me: saved my soul, been with me constantly, given me loving parents and family, given me resources and health, given me a church family and the list is without end.

Even now, you continue each day to bless me with your loving presence, but your most costly blessing is my salvation.

After saying that, I still ask you to help me trust you more and more. Grow my faith so that when "times of trouble" come, I may thank you for that too. (James 1:2-4). Because you are sovereign, you can bring good out of everything. (Romans 8:28). Draw me close to you as I go through today.

I am yours; therefore, my cares and concerns are yours. I pray Joshua 24:15. Oh, how I love you, Lord!

*Starting
Another Day
with You*

— *Day 1* —

Oh, Lord, how thankful I am that I can come directly to you asking for forgiveness, help, strength, guidance, courage. You were tempted in every way, just like I am (Hebrews 4:14, 16) yet you did not sin. I have sinned; but because you went to the cross, I can come to you as I am right now—to the Throne of Grace. It is here I find mercy and grace that gives me hope and encouragement to start another day—even if I failed you miserably yesterday. Thank you, Lord.

I am yours; you chose me. It is you who justifies me. It is you who is interceding for me there at the right hand of God. (Romans 8:33-34). You have clothed me in a robe of righteousness (Isaiah 61:10) that you bought with your blood. Our Father only sees me as blameless because of your sacrifice on the cross and, therefore, there is no condemnation for me. Thank you. Thank you. And, I can go to His throne with you anytime. I don't have to carry that guilt throughout the year waiting for a high priest to make a sacrifice. You have already paid it all!

With all that said, Lord, I still have difficulty keeping my focus on you. Help me. My desire is to be aware of your presence continually. I want to please you. Help me block distractions as I come to you. This time with you is precious; make the world go away.

I reaffirm my decision and pray Joshua 24:15. Draw me and each of my house closer to you.

Love, honor, praise and thanksgiving all belong to you!

— *Day 2* —

One more time, thank you, Lord, for being here with me in the quiet morning hours. Especially thank you for not being repulsed by my neediness. May I grow strong in your light; dependent on you, yes! close to you, yes! yielded to you, yes! allowing your Power to flow into me. Thank you, Lord!

"You are gracious and righteous. You are full of compassion." You saved my soul and you have saved me over and over—even when I wasn't aware of this continual process at the time. You are and have been so good to me. (Psalm 116: 5-7 and I say Amen).

Lord, give me courage to thank you during the hard time—pain, disappointment, etc. Help me learn to give thanks for everything. (Ephesians 5:20). I want to yield myself to your will as evidence of my trust in you. "In quietness and trust is my strength." (Isaiah 30:15). All I know—without you, I am nothing!

The storms of life make it easy to lose sight of the hope that is available to me in you, Lord. You are my anchor and you hold. You never leave me. The storm may continue, but you are with me every step of the way. ***Through it all!***

Help me stay focused on you and not on the "waves of the storm." I want to keep a heavenly/heavenward, eternal perspective in the midst of it all. There is more to living than life here, and you have allowed even that to be good. I have been blessed! And one of these days I will see you Face to face. That will be glory! (Romans 8:18).

Until I take my last breath or until you return in your glory, my decision is to serve you. (Joshua 24:15). Today make me aware of those you would have me touch in your name. I have failed you; forgive me, Lord.

— *Day 3* —

Lord, I am repeating. Thank you for this time alone with you before I really start the day. Lord, you know I have to walk Aries...so as I pass the coffee pot, I have to stop for that first cup...but I haven't started my day until I talk with you. Nothing compares to this time. Paul said he considered everything else as rubbish when he made a comparison. (Philippians 3:7-8).

I find it easy to bring my joys to you and say "Thank you." Help me bring my disappointments to you and just as easily say "Thank you" for them. Remind me to come to you when something messes up my plans and my desires. Bringing my cares to you will not only bless me immediately but will also at the same time build a stronger on-going relationship with you. May I learn to see each disappointment as an opportunity to view a situation from your perspective.

Teach me, Lord. Train me. Help me submit and totally surrender to you. Romans 12:10 tells me to "Show family affection with brotherly love...outdoing one another in showing honor." In my new family here at Buckner, I want to learn to do that so that you may be glorified. May I always look to you, who humbled yourself, left your throne in glory, and came to this earth to die for sinners like me. When my focus is on you, may I find ways to shower others with brotherly love and acts of kindness.

My decision is still in place today: Joshua 24:15. Hold me and each of my family close to you, guarding and guiding our paths.

Love, honor, praise and thanksgiving belong to you.

— Day 4 —

Lord, thank you for allowing me to walk in peace with you today—all day, one step at a time, (Exodus 33:64; Psalm 29:11). Lord, you knew you were headed for the cross and you never faltered; you just kept putting one foot in front of the other—healing, teaching, disciplining, and loving as you went.

Help me keep my mind on your presence with me; I know the more demanding my day, the more I can depend on you, the more I can expect from you. You are the "iron and bronze at my protective gates," (Deuteronomy 33:25), and you will give me the strength I need today. Thank you for the challenging times that wake me up and show me how totally dependent I am on you. You will "equip me with everything good for doing your will." (Hebrews 13:20-21).

Lord, thank you for your Word: Isaiah 54:4-5. When I am tired, I can hear the devil—Satan himself—saying, "Shame on you." Your Word is true and he is a liar. I no longer need to carry the shame of my youth or the sadness of being alone. You are my constant companion and your blood covers the misdeeds of my past. When I humbly bring my present failings to you, you lovingly tell me "to go and sin no more." Shame distorts who I am in you. Shame keeps me from trusting your grace, enjoying forgiveness, and resting in restoration. It keeps me blinded to all the blessings you bought for me at the cross and the empty grave.

I want to trust you totally just as the woman at the well did. (John 4:5-7).

I love, praise, and honor you and Joshua 24:15 is my decision today.

— *Day 5* —

Lord, thank you for this time with you. I repeat a condensed version of some of your promises, but I love hearing them. Paul tells me to "learn the secret of being content in any and every situation. (Philippians 4:12). I haven't gotten there yet, but it's my goal, Lord."

You tell me "You are with me and watch over me wherever I go..." (Genesis 28:15). When I say that out loud and know you meant that for me as well as for Jacob, I am truly safe and secure.

Paul was in prison when he confirms "My God will meet all your needs according to his glorious riches in Christ Jesus." I want to know all about you and how you provide for me out of your abundance—even in the midst of chaos. I want to put all my energy into trusting you and enjoying your presence. I don't want my circumstances to determine the quality of my life. I am resting on (counting on, betting on) you to teach me how "to be content in any and every situation." And, I am not in prison.

Lee says "You are with me and will watch over me wherever I go. You will meet all my needs according to your glorious riches. And, best of all, nothing in all creation will be able to separate me from your love." My decision is the same this a.m. as it was yesterday...Joshua 24:15. Bind Satan from me and each of my family.

Love you! Praise you! Honor you, Lord!

— Day 6 —

Early a.m. Lord, what would I do without you, your Word? You are going to do a brand new thing. You have already begun! Though I don't see it yet, you will make a road through the wilderness for _____ to come home and create rivers for him/her as he/she is in this desert. (Isaiah 43:19). Lord, you know whose name I am putting in the blank.

Lord, just as you rescued me from the dominion of darkness and brought me into the kingdom of the Son in whom I have redemption and forgiveness of sin, (Colossians 1:13-14) I am asking you to rescue_____.

Lord, you tell me and I believe you that "If I abide in you and your words abide in me, I can ask anything and it shall be done." I know _____ has free will and choices, but I am asking you to continue drawing him/her to you. Nothing is as strong as your love. (John 15:7).

Lord, just as Paul was persuaded that nothing—not death, not life, not angels or principalities, nothing in the present, not things to come, not height, not depth, not anything created—can separate _____ from your love; I am persuaded also! Your love, Lord, and the love of the Father (Romans 8:38-39) is greater than all else.

Lord, I am truly humbling myself before you, under your mighty hand, asking you to lift _____ out of the pit he/she is in. I am bringing you my concerns for him/her because I know you are always thinking about your children, especially me and each of my family this morning. You are watching everything that concerns each of us. (1 Peter 5:6-7).

Lord, I am praying that _____ will love you with all his/her heart, all his/her soul, all his/her mind, and all his/her strength.

Continued on page 122...

...Continued from page 121

(Mark 12:30). May _____ seek you with all his/her heart. Give him/her discernment. (Jeremiah 29:13).

Lord, I am asking you to give _____ a new heart and put a new spirit in him/her. Remove his/her heart of stone and give him/her a heart of flesh. (Ezekiel 36:26). Only you are capable of that.

Lord, teach _____; show him/her vividly that the body is your temple, that you live in him/her and have lived in him/her since he/she accepted you as a personal Savior. (1 Corinthians 6:19).

Lord, help _____be strong and courageous and not be afraid. Remind him/her that you go with him/her, never leave him/her, and never forsake him/her. (Deuteronomy 31:6).

Lord, your arm is not too short to save_____ from this mess he/she is in and your ear is not too dull to hear my cry for him/her. (Isaiah 59:1).

Lord, I will not be downcast over this situation that those I love are involved in; I will not despair. My hope is in you and I will praise you. You are my Savior and my God. (Psalm 42:5-6).

Lord, "though the fig tree does not bud and there are no grapes on the vines; through there are no sheep in the pen and no cattle in the stalls", though _____chooses to go his/her own way, I will rejoice in you. I will be joyful in you, my God and my Savior. You are my strength. (Habakkuk 3 :17-19).

Lord, I will give thanks in all circumstances for that is your will for me since I am in you and your Spirit lives in me. (1 Thessalonians 5:18). I will give thanks in these circumstances.

Continued on page 123...

...Continued from page 122

Lord, hear my cries tonight and in your name I am asking that Satan be bound. You are victorious; you have the final say! Guard me and each of my family physically, spiritually, emotionally, mentally, and financially. Send your mighty angels to be a hedge along our paths and protect all our steps. Fill each of us with blessing, health, safety, guidance, and purpose. Cause us to hear your voice and walk in your steps holding your hand. Use us for your glory.

May I just be still and know you are God. You will be exalted among all nations on earth. (Psalm 46:10).

— Day 6 — Yes still day 6.

Lord, it is you, your Holy Spirit, and your Word that gives comfort when the disappointments are almost too intense to bear. This time with you is the best part of my day—and the next best time is that time just before I turn off the light to rest for the night. In that time I am thanking you for the blessings I've received from you during my waking hours.

Lord, I want to please you in all that I do and say—seeking you above all else. May each decision—not just major ones but each one—be to glorify you. When I am living in close communion with you, the decision making is easier. When I am aware of your presence, I can almost instinctively know what pleases you. Not always, but almost. May I delight myself in you more and more and seek your pleasure in all I do. (Psalm 37:4).

There are times when it seems as though "things" will never get better and there is no light at the end of the tunnel. But, Lord, I know you are always present even when I don't see or feel your presence—even when circumstances remain exactly the same.

You are always showing me how much you love me and reminding me you will never leave me. You do minister to me specifically and personally—even when I don't sense it. You come in a variety of ways when I need your love and tenderness the most. Today I will take time to turn to you, look for you, and listen for you.

My decision is still the same: Joshua 24:15. Love, honor, and praise with thanksgiving belong to you.

— *Day 7* —

Lord, thank you for this predawn time out here on the patio with you. What a blessing! It is delightful. You do give special gifts; and the most special one is your presence with me. All true beauty reflects who you are—and this morning I see peace.

Help me become a "thing of beauty" reflecting you. Work out your plan for me, within me. Clear out all the debris and clutter so there is room for your Spirit to take full possession. Help me carefully take care of all the blessings you have put in my hands; but help me cheerfully let go of anything you choose to take away. You are omniscient; you know what I need. You are omnipotent; you continue providing all I need—abundantly. You are omnipresent and you love me. (Psalm 29:2). I want to give you the glory you are due.

Lord, I have asked you to grow my trust and faith. I really want to grow, but the learning process is painful. Just as getting rid of "most of my stuff" and downsizing from "830" was painful, so is getting rid of the clutter and debris within me. Seeing **MY** hopes disintegrate, feeling the disappointments, fearing the immediate future as though you weren't there with me—that's what I need to clear out of my life. All that belongs to you and I need to leave it in your hands. I need to grow in trust and faith. You did not put me in charge.

You have already begun a "new thing" in answer to my prayers. I don't see it yet, but I thank you. (Isaiah 49:13). You do provide a path home and create rivers in the desert. Thank you.

Joshua 24:15 remains my prayer and I am asking you to bind Satan from me and each of my family. All love, honor, and praise are due you.

— *Day 8* —

Lord, thank you for your sovereignty. You are in total control of this chaotic world and I can be at peace with that. I am so thankful you never change and are forever. (Psalm 102:27). Thank you for your grace that is overflowing and freely available.

I want to live in grace—to go about my daily responsibilities fully aware of your love, mercy, and presence with me. Let my life be a manifestation of the freedom you give—may my actions be based on faith, not fear—may I be obedient to you and an imitation of you. I am definitely flawed, but I want to function with your power within me.

Lord, I live here with no significant responsibilities and yet there are times I don't make room for you in my day—or cut the time short. You told Martha (Luke 41-42) only one thing was necessary—communing with you. Jesus, you were physically in Martha's house and she thought "household duties" were more important than spending time with you. Lord, I want there to be nothing more important to me than you—yet my actions would often indicate otherwise.

You live within me and I am constantly in your presence! I want to be aware of you. Let me—help me—be ready to love and serve those I come in contact with today. Let me be your hands, feet, ears, and voice. Use me.

My decision is still Joshua 24:15 and my prayers are for me and my family to follow close to you.

— *Day 9* —

Lord, thank you for being the Alpha and the Omega! Help me remember to thank you for all you are in between. Help me learn to appreciate the difficult days, say thank you, and be stimulated by the challenges. May I gain confidence from my relationship with you now, from your Word and its promises, and from my memories of how faithful you have been in the past. (Isaiah 41:10). And, Lord, you remain the same! (Psalm 102:27). I change, my circumstances change, but you never change! Hallelujah!

In you, Lord, I live, and more than that: I have my being! I am your child! (Acts 17:28).

Thank you for loving me beyond my comprehension and for equipping me to be your hands and feet. "Now to You who is able to do above and beyond all that I ask and think," (Ephesians3:20), I praise you. Lord, I don't know the answer(s), but you do. And I will trust you.

Open my eyes to see as you work miracles in answer to my prayers so I may praise you even more. Open my eyes to see the opportunity(ies) you provide for me to be a blessing to others and give me the willingness to take the steps to be what you want me to be.

Remove anything/everything in my life that might keep you from answering my urgent prayers. Lord, I am asking you and the Father to bind Satan from me and each of my family. We need you with us now. Joshua 24:15. Again love, honor, praise, thanksgiving belong to you.

— *Day 10* —

Lord, give me the desire to walk in your Spirit today and every day. May my entire being be focused on living in your presence—completely enveloped in your love and peace. (Galatians 5:16-18).

Changing one thing (removing one sin) won't make me be like you, but wanting to be like you can determine every step I take to be like you. And, I want you to transform all of me to be like you. (Romans 12:2).

As I move from this quiet time into the activities of this day, help me keep this awareness of your presence. You are omniscient; you know what's going on across our nation and of the chaos in my family. Thank you for your sovereignty, your omnipotence! You are omnipresent; may we all be aware that you are Immanuel, God with us! And, you are a God of love!

Help me keep **you** in the picture as I visualize tomorrow, next week, next year or I will sin against you. (Luke 12:22-25). I would be consumed with worry. You are with me at all times and with those I love. Your promises are for them just as they are for me. (Deuteronomy 31:6). Help them—especially those dear to me become more and more aware of you and all that you are.

Lord, I am praying 2 Corinthians 10:5 for me and each of my family. Then I am asking you to bind Satan from us as I pray Joshua 24:15. All this "help me, give me" and not once have I said "thank you" for all that you have already done. I do thank you—love you—honor you—and praise you!

— *Day 11* —

Lord, as I start today, I am remembering that you are omniscient and know what today holds. You are my omnipotent Savior who loves me and will empower me to meet today in ways that glorify you. You are omnipresent so I am never alone. A quiet "thank you" is hardly enough! (Ephesians 1: 18-20).

The degree to which you strengthen me doesn't depend on your ability but on the difficulty of the situation and my willingness to depend on you for help—my trust level. Lord, increase my trust level. May I always look to you and your strength; seeking your face in every situation. (Psalm 105:4). You are my strength. (Deuteronomy 33:25).

Just as I can't expect a healthier life style by removing one item (bread), I can't just walk with you sometimes and then expect to bear fruit in my life. (Galatians 5:22-23). I want you in every area of my life; I want to be immersed in your will.

May I fix my mind on you always. May my feet walk in your footprints. May my hands serve as yours did. May I see and hear you as you guide l me. Lord, I am yours.

Joshua 24:15 is my prayer and I am lifting each of my family up to you to be filled with your love, strength, courage, peace, guidance—and a desire to know you more. (Give Kristina comfort today.) It is in your name that I am also asking that Satan be bound from us that we may glorify you. Love, honor, praise and thanks go to you.

— *Day 12* —

Truly , Lord, "My cup runneth over." My blessings from you are beyond measure. (Psalm 23:5). I don't deserve any of the "abundant life" (John 10:10) that you came to give me. Your kingdom is not about deserving; it is about believing and receiving. Help me develop a grateful heart and receive every gift in joyful harmony with you. (Roman 8:32)).

How often I have been so upset about what I thought you were withholding from me!! When I have thought like that, I failed to see your blessings. When I let my mind be controlled by **the things I see**—circumstances, relationships, preconceived ideas—I miss seeing your hand at work. Until I let go of my views, my sin, my presumptions and start governing my mind around your Word, I will miss out on so many blessings.

Yet, when I intentionally make the effort to meet with you each morning, to control my thoughts and to take them captive to your Word, I am at peace. (Romans 8:6). Thank you for being with me this morning. Thank you for helping me reset my mind from things that will hurt me and set it toward your Word that will lead me to life and peace.

Joshua 24:15 is my prayer again this morning. Guard, guide, and hold me and each of my family close to you this day. Bind Satan from us, Lord.

I love, honor, and praise you.

— *Day 13* —

Lord, you are my "hope of glory." You are the one who walks beside me, who holds my hand, and who lives within me. As I sit here with you, in this quiet, early morning hour, I am very aware of your presence. (Oh, to be able to hold onto ***that awareness*** as I go through the day. Colossians 1:27).

When I am aware of your presence, it is then that I know joy and peace. Lord, I want to bubble over (overflow) with this joy and peace that comes from you alone. Only in your power is this possible; only when I am fully trusting you. (Romans 15:13)

There were "things to be done—work to be accomplished for you—and I got caught up in getting it done, which was a good thing: e.g. I kept a clean house, a pretty yard, cooked healthy meals, etc. (Titus 2:5). But, Lord, so often I failed to keep a loving, gracious spirit towards others, especially those closest to me. Forgive me, Lord! Since I can't change the past, help me be what you want me to be ***today,*** loving each of your children that I meet. A good thing can turn sinful if I fail to love others as I accomplish the task...even the task you want done.

The way I do something is more important than what I do, Lord. Why did it take me so long to learn that? May everything I do be done in love, mercy, faith, justice. (Matthew 23:1-12, 23-24). I want to be like you, Lord. Keep me aware of my heart's attitude even when I do good things.

Today, I again pray for forgiveness where I loved my family imperfectly, selfishly. Give me an opportunity to love them and others as you want them loved. Plant and grow your fruit—love, joy, peace, patience, kindness, goodness, faithfulness, gentleness, and self-control—in me and in them. (Galatians 5:22-23).

— *Day 14* —

Lord, before all else—I thank you, praise you, honor you and love you for who you are, my Lord and Savior—and for all the blessings you continue to give me.

"Love one another." (John 13:34). This morning I can sit here and know I am fully understood and loved unconditionally. You have cleansed me, made me radiantly righteous. (2 Corinthians 5:21). You see me as I will be when I get to heaven—not as I am today. You did all that—not me. And you left your Spirit within me to bring about a transformation day after day. Now that's a **bona fide** miracle!

May I continue to be aware of my dependence on you throughout the day. Oh! how often I have been just like the Pharisees who knew the Word—even followed the law—but didn't embody your Spirit. I have often been critical and judgmental instead of loving and encouraging. Forgive me.

Lord, help me remember it's not about what we do, but about who you are and what you have done for us. Thank you for continuing to remind me again and again of the gospel, the good news. All of us need you; and as Christians we should be known by our love (John 13:35) for you and for each other.

You even tell me *how* and *why* I am to love others—because you first loved me. It is through your powerful love that I am to love others. You loved me when I was rebellious and cruel; help me to love others the same way you loved me. I want to be loving as you are loving.

Joshua 24:15 is my decision again this a.m. Hear my cry for you to bind Satan from us. In your name, I pray.

— *Day 15* —

Lord, thank you for another day, more time to learn and relearn the lessons you have for me. It is so easy to thank you and praise you when all is going just the way I want them to. That's no lesson. But, when something goes awry—different from the way I planned or the way I wanted—I have to relearn the lesson: "Give thanks in everything." (1 Thessalonians 5:18).

David prayed and prayed for his baby son to live (2 Samuel 12:16-23); but when he knew the baby was dead—he washed, changed clothes, and went to the Tabernacle to worship. (No wonder he was a man after your own heart.) Help me be that same kind of example for others.

Let me bring every desire, care, and concern to you. When you answer "yes," let me praise you with my whole being. When you tell me "no, not yet, or I have something better," let me accept your answer with grace and immediately worship you with my whole being. Your way is always perfect!

I thank you for your constant faithfulness. Truly, I want to learn to live in gratitude in every situation—despite the outcome. Teach me how to do that—to be that! I know you are worthy of my thanksgiving and praise.

When a situation begins to control my thoughts, remind me to bring it to you, talk to you about it, see it in the Light of Your Presence. There will always be trouble, but more importantly: "You will always be with me." (John 16:33 and Psalm 89:15).

Joshua 24:15 is still my decision and prayer. Guard and guide each of my family—me too. Love, honor, and praise go to you.

— *Day 16* —

Lord, my vocabulary is so limited and my literary style is nonexistent so I simply start this day repeating what I have already told you over and over. Lord, I do love you. This quiet time is the best part of my day; here there is peace and refreshment. I am thankful that you—Creator of the universe—are here with me.

David may have been sensing this same thing as he looked at the day ahead: "Where will my help come from? My help comes from the Lord, the Maker of heaven and earth." (Psalm 121:1-2). I don't attempt to compare myself to David who was a man after your own heart, but his words reminded me just how blessed I am to be in the presence of One who has all power and who wants me to seek his face throughout the day.

When I look ahead, I see a twisted, complicated situation that could go in any direction. I cannot prepare for all the possibilities; I know I can't; I tried for years and always failed. Today I know where my help is: "You hold me with your hand, you guide me with counsel; you are always with me, and will take me on into glory." (Psalm 73:23-24).

Help me take advantage of all this as I remember that although you inhabit all space all the time, you communicate with me only in the present. My help comes from you.

My decision is still Joshua 24:15, and I ask you to hold me and each of my family close to you. I cry for you to bind Satan from us.

— *Day 17* —

Lord, yes, thank you for being my Lord! Thank you for taking away my condemnation when you went to the cross for me. (Romans 8:1-2). Thank you for setting me free and for staying with me to guide me each day in each situation. (Isaiah 30:21).

Thank you for being my Shepherd who provides green pastures, quiet waters, and restoration. (Psalm 23:1-3). I am your sheep; I want to hear your voice, know it is you, and follow you. (John 10:27). But, I am truly a sheep that does need constant care, guidance, protection; otherwise, I do dumb things! Thank you for taking me up in your arms, holding me close, talking to me, calming me. Oh! What a Shepherd you are!

Today, I affirm (reaffirm) my decision to serve you: Joshua 24:15. If there is something in me that would keep anyone in my family (or anyone else, period) from desiring to serve you, reveal it to me so that I can come to you asking you to remove it from me.

Again, today I pray that I and each of my family will walk in intense love for you, reverently fearing your holy name and loving our neighbors as ourselves. And, at this moment, I am using the power of your holy name to bind Satan from me and my family. We are yours and the Father's, and we need your protection.

Love, honor, praise, and thanksgiving all go to you.

— *Day 18* —

Lord, as I lean dependently on you, you give me peace and I feel complete. Yes, in you, I am complete! I don't have to figure everything out on my on; you are the omniscient one.

Thank you for your love letter to me. I want to know all that is in it. Some parts are so special—so "just for me"—that I have to go back to them over and over. Some I have "written on my heart" so they are always with me—and as David said "so that I won't sin against you." I want to live as you designed me to live—in close communion with you.

You sent your Holy Spirit to live within me; yes, I know my body is your temple. (I Corinthians 6:19-20). I try to take good care of it for you as it does not belong to me. You bought me with your blood. Lord, I want to care for my heart and soul as well. Your Word heals and strengthens my mind. Help me grow closer to you; guard my heart and mind. (Philippians 4:6-7).

Lord, help me stop pulling the old "I'll solve-it-myself trick." Help me submit to your will completely and accept things exactly as they are at this moment—then give thanks. I have only two commandments I must keep: love you and love my neighbor as myself. I want to do that so your love flows through me—fully aware that I am dependent on you, trusting you.

Joshua 24:15 is still my prayer and thank you for binding Satan from each of my family.

— *Day 19* —

Thank you, Lord, for choosing me to live this life with you. Thank you for your deep love and concern for me. I want to learn to be more and more like you each day; help me practice the tenderhearted mercy and kindness you have shown me. (Colossians 3:12).

Today is an adventure, with you as my Guide and my Companion. I want to stay in step with you, aware of your presence, getting to know you more deeply. I really want to know you before I get to heaven where I will truly be with you all the time. I don't want us to be strangers when I get there.

Lord, help me hurry when you hurry, climb when you climb, and rest when you rest. I want to enjoy the rhythm of a life aware of your constant presence. Help me focus on the path just ahead of me—as I hold your hand. (Psalm 27:13-14). Thank you for your unfailing love as you lead me in this adventure and for strength as you show me the final destination. (Exodus 15:13).

Thank you, thank you, thank you! Help me learn to give thanks in everything as that is your will for me. (1 Thessalonians 5:18).

My decision remains the same: Joshua 24:15. Hold me and each of my family close to you—guarding our hearts and minds. And, I just keep on asking you to bind Satan from each of us.

All love, praise, honor go to you this morning.

— *Day 20* —

Lord, thank you for this time with you. Thank you that out of your glorious riches you give me strength over and over through your Spirit who lives within me. May I be so rooted and established in your love that I can grasp just how "deep and wide" your love is. Though I don't understand, I accept that your love is unconditional and I ask that you fill me with it. (Ephesians 3:16-19).

Thank you for allowing me to simply pour out my heart to you and grow in trust because you are my refuge. (Psalm 62:8). Thank you for your gift of salvation. I didn't and couldn't earn it; it was your ***gift***— your gift of faith! (Ephesians 2:8-9).

Today and in the immediate days ahead, help me, Lord, to be your instrument. Let your love—not mine—flow through me to heal wounds in this family's relationships. Now may the God of hope fill me with all joy and peace as I trust in him—and you, Lord—so others may find hope and peace also. (Romans 15:13).

So many situations are not the ones I would choose to use growing my faith and trust; but you, Lord, can do miracles and my faith is growing. You have made so many scriptures come alive as I watch what seems to be hopeless tendencies change. Thank you for the miracles you have already begun in our lives. Use me as you will and keep me out of your way when I am not the one you choose to use.

My decision: Joshua 24:15 still stands. Bind Satan from us, Lord, that we may be a glory to you. Love, praise, honor belong to you. (Lord, you know that is not just a meaningless comment I make each day; I mean every word of it.)

— *Day 21* —

Lord, it's Thanksgiving week—but then you already knew that, didn't you? I want every week of what's left of my life to be a thanksgiving week—every day—all the time. I'm starting the list with "I'm thankful for your Presence and your Peace." (Matthew 28:20 and Luke 24:36). You yourself said you were always with me and that gives me peace. With thanksgiving and praise, I can be in a "new and improved" relationship with you, thus allowing your riches to flow into me—to overflowing so others may have hope through your power. (Romans 15:3).

Lord, you are holy beyond comprehension, even though you walked this earth as a human. Yes, I want to be holy—but not "holier-than-thou." Forgive me for the times, I have held that attitude and replace that attitude with a "wholesome fear of God." I want to be set apart for your use. (2 Corinthians 7:1). I want to reflect who you are; I want to draw others to you.

Help me know what holiness looks like here—today—in my life. Show me how that looks in action. Expose any behavior I need to change. Help me recognize my own sinfulness; I want to be compassionate to others as I practice purity in my thoughts, my words, and my actions. Teach me, Lord.

Joshua 24:15 is my prayer and I ask you to bind Satan from me and each of my family.

Love, honor, praise, thanksgiving go to you.

— *Day 22* —

Heavenly Father, I come to you this morning in your Son Jesus' name asking forgiveness for all sin—but especially—the one that I just keep on committing—over and over. For my relationship with you to grow, I must agree with you about what sin is and I do. Forgive me and may I find strength not to fail you again—not sin against you again. In your Son I can find peace about this. (Philippians 4:7); I do trust him.

Paul says "I will boast all the more about my weakness so that Christ's power may reside in me." (2 Corinthians 12:9). I don't know that I fully understand your message to me here. I just want to confess my weakness and find the strength in you and through the Holy Spirit that lives within me to live in harmony with you. I am back to my "go-to" prayer: "Help me, Jesus."

Lord, I know you don't love me because I am perfect; you love me because I believe you are the Son of God—the Messiah—who is perfect and who wrapped me in his robe of righteousness. I am asking for your empowering grace to give me strength to live a daily life that pleases you.

Thank you for hearing my cry (my cries). I know you hear me and you are able to do all and more than I ask. (Ephesians 3:20). My prayer continues to be Joshua 24:15. You are all powerful so it is in your name I am asking you to bind Satan from me and my family so that we may glorify you.

— Day 23 —

Lord, you are good and you do what is good; teach me your statues. (Psalm 119:68). Your ways are perfect and your Word is pure, (Psalm 18:30) and you shield me as I take refuge in you. You give grace and glory; you don't withhold good from those who live with integrity. (Psalm 84:11). And all this is reason enough to be thankful.

Your Word is my reality about who you are—the Son of God. My reality is not my circumstances around me. I have no reason to complain about anything and I want to be like Habakkuk in 3:17-18. May I always be joyful in you, Lord—not sometimes, under some circumstances—but always.

With a thankful attitude, I can come to you and see through the windows of heaven to get glimpses of Glory. May I learn the language of Love; it's the language you speak, Lord.

As I sit here, quietly in your presence, fill me completely—both my heart and mind—with thankfulness. When I think of the love you poured out to me on the cross, I am in awe. Nothing separates me from that love. (Romans 8:38-39). And, each day I continue to find gifts that you left specifically for me—it's better than Christmas!

Lord, today I reaffirm my decision to serve you; (Joshua 24:15) and I ask you to bind Satan from me and my family just as you bound him when he tempted you. Make him flee from us. Love, honor, praise go to you.

— *Day 24* —

Lord, I'm late in coming to you today, but I do love you. I am especially thankful for your special blessing of the season with family. You amaze me in the ways you continue to show up in my life. I never want to lose perspective of that: you are always present.

Help me learn to give thanks to you in every situation (Ephesians 5:20) as I want to be obedient to you. I especially want to give thanks because your love endures forever. (Psalm 118:1). And, I want to walk with you and acclaim you—not just today but every day.

I want to learn to give thanks regardless of my feelings about a situation, because I get "the best end of that deal." You give me joy regardless of my circumstances. I may be in the same situation with nothing changed, but I thank you as you have begun to help me be more open to your plan—your perspective.

Lord, I don't want to be a complainer. Help me praise you for who you are, for the gift of salvation that you gave me, and for each of the daily blessings that come from you—life, family, friends, breath, sight, hearing, food, shelter, and the list goes on.

Joshua 24:15 is still my prayer. Thank you for binding Satan from me and my family that we may glorify you.

Love, honor, praise and thanks go to you.

— *Day 25* —

Yes, Lord, I am thankful that you—a majestic, sovereign God—Creator of the universe—would allow me to spend time alone with you. Thank you for your continual, constant presence; and may my prayers of thanksgiving be as constant as your presence.

Lord, you know me. I bring my cares to you and hold onto them with all my strength—not giving them to you—as I say "Hurry, Lord, fix this mess." David asked you to do the same thing. (Psalm 70:1-3). If I don't let you have my cares, it is not a prayer of trust; it is just my saying "I want things fixed my way and I know you are able and sovereign. But I'll hold onto them."

Help me grow closer to you, deeper in you, more like you each day as I look for your will in my life. May my knowledge of your sufficiency develop to maturity. You are the God of hope; fill me to overflowing with joy and peace as I trust in you so others may have hope in **your** power, not mine. (Romans 15:13).

My Joshua 24:15 decision remains today and I pray I will become the kind of worshiper you seek—one who worships in spirit and truth. (John 4:23-24). Forgive me of my lack of trust—Lord, grow it **NOW!** (Big smile).

Love, trust, and honor—as well as praise and thanksgiving—belong to you.

— *Day 26* —

Lord, again this morning I look around and see an unending list of blessings you have provided for me. Help me not only **be** grateful to you, but also **show** that gratitude as I go about this day. May others see you in me.

You did make this beautiful fall day and I do rejoice in it. (Psalm 118:24). But, Lord, if this day were cold, grey, gloomy I would still need to rejoice in it because you would have made it too! I want to see you in every day—in everything; you are omnipresent—always there. For that, I am thankful and can rejoice.

This world is not perfect—blessings and disappointments come on the same day! Help me thank you for both. Help me share the blessings and grow closer to you—grow deeper in you—through the disappointments. Help me remember your promise to work all things for my good. (Romans 8:28). I have no reason to worry or complain; I am yours.

You have set me free—I want to learn to live in this radical freedom you have given me. I want to live freely in you—with my mind fixed firmly, steadfastly on you. Teach me to be your sheep—simply listening for your voice, following contentedly after you. (John 10:27).

This day just let your love flow through me at each encounter with your other sheep—each person I meet. When I write Joshua 24:15, you know the prayers that go with that code word. Without you, I am nothing.

Love, honor, praise and thanksgiving go to you.

— *Day 27* —

Lord, each time I come to you in the quiet early morning hours, I am more amazed at the blessings you have for me—both heavenly and earthly. And, each time I look at the true abundance of your riches, I am awed that you allow me access to them. I am just learning how to say "Thank you" for all things and I need to learn to say "Hallelujah" for them too. (Revelation 19:3-6). Hallelujah seems to be the language of heaven.

Help me learn to trust you completely—instead of trying to control. I want to focus on you so I can see what you are doing. Help me center my entire being in You. You created me in your image and that's how I want to live—in You.

You came that I would have abundant life. (John 10:10). May I be so aware of just how abundant this life in you is that I continually overflow with praise and thankfulness. May my life be a journey with a deep consciousness of you: a journey of joy, obedience, unity, readiness, nurturing, encouragement, and yielding.

May I concentrate on these things today—not tomorrow or next week, but today! Joshua 24:15 is again my decision and prayer. Guide and keep us all—drawing us closer and closer to you.

My love, praise, honor, and thanksgiving go to you, Lord.

— *Day 28* —

Lord, you are omniscipant—all wise; not just omniscient—all knowing, but also omniscipant—all wise. And your Word tells me, "Wisdom is supreme—so get wisdom and whatever else I get, get understanding." (Proverbs 4:7-8). You add that I am to "cherish wisdom and she will exalt me."

Lord, as I study your Word and its truths, teach me how to apply them to my life and in my circumstances. Teach me when to be silent and when to speak; when to listen and respond with grace. Help me recall your precious promises and see your reassurances that are not readily obvious. Help me discern right from wrong. And, Lord, I never want to lose my focus of your loving sacrifice on the cross for me. May I always look with awe and respect at God, the Father, as the ultimate authority.

Lord, I do want wisdom and you tell me (James 1:5) that when I ask as a believer I will receive it. You know me; I want it now. Help me be patient and wait for your perfect timing—but I do believe you will give it to me. (2 Chronicles 1:10-12).

And now, Lord, I simply rest in your unfailing love. I simply bring my body, spirit, and mind to you for restoration. My cares are yours. (1 Peter 5:7). Today, I will rejoice in your marvelous love that is beyond measure. (Ephesians 3:16-19).

What else can I do but bring you my thanks and gratitude. You are my Lord and Provider—Protector and Sustainer!

Joshua 24:15—Bind Satan from me and each of my family that we may glorify you.

All love, honor, and praise belong to you.

— *Day 29* —

Lord, only you can bring peace to the depth of my heart and soul.

As I sit here in your presence, I want to be totally open to you and all the blessings you provide—including your reproof.

I can tell you I didn't kill or steal or since we last talked, but I don't want any of my "small sins" to hinder my relationship with you. I know you will forgive them as soon as I bring them to you. Reveal them to me so there are no dark desires within me. Enlighten me with your goodness, Lord.

It is through faith in you and your love that I will get to heaven to be with you forever (Ephesians 2:8-9), but I thank you for faith that brings heaven—your presence—to my soul today. Faith is the assurance of things hoped for (Hebrews 11:1) and I am certain you are here with me now.

You will guide me always as I allow you to; you will satisfy all my needs and give me strength for this day (Isaiah 58:11); you have never failed me. As I look back, I have failed you often; but you have never failed me or left me alone. You have patiently waited with open arms for me to come to you. How can I ever doubt you!!!

Without you, I am nothing. Without you and your love flowing through me to others, I am a "noise-maker." (1 Corinthians 13:1-7). When others see me, I want them to say: "She looks like her Daddy. You can tell she's his child."

Joshua 24:15: my decision today. Hold me and my house close to you. Gather us up in your arms and carry each of us close to your heart. (Isaiah 40:11).

Love, praise, honor and thanksgiving go to you.

— *Day 30* —

Lord, thank you for this day, this time with you. You created me; your blood saved me; you gave me new life; and you planned work for me to do for you. (Ephesians 2:10). Give me strength and courage to do that—as well as discernment to recognize your plan. I want to be your co-worker. (1 Corinthians 3:9). May I be obedient and follow you wherever you lead. (Psalm 32:8).

This is your world—you are sovereign. Help me remember that even though evil seems so strong; you are the victorious ruler. Problems are an inescapable part of this world; and I can go into "fix it" mode automatically, acting as though I am God—without even consulting you. Forgive me; may my relationship with you be my top priority. Remind me to talk to you and get your perspective, guidance, and permission first. (Matthew 6:33).

I do want to see, hear, and know your plan; I am only a co-worker here on earth! And my citizenship is in heaven—but I do have my "green card" to work for you here. (Philippians 3:20). Lord, you are faithful. May I be transformed as you want me to be.

Instead of my trying to fix everything to my liking—and everything that comes to my attention—help me wait on you and let you show me what is important to you and what you have planned for me to do! I am only a co-worker, not the boss! Help me remember that.

Joshua 24:15. You are faithful; you will strengthen me and protect me from the evil one. (2 Thessalonians 3:3). I am binding Satan from me and my family—in your name, Lord, not mine. You are due all my love, honor, and praise this day.

— Day 31 —

Thank you for this TAG! You came to die for me. The Holy Spirit lives in me and my Father in heaven watches over me. What a way to start new day...aware of your presence and all the blessings you bring!

Lord, you know I had a good earthly father—as well as a wonderful mother—but you are the perfect Father. You have provided and continue to provide for my every need—and you are always with me. (Romans 8:38-39). Yes, nothing can separate me from your love. Because of my relationship with Jesus Christ, the Son of God, I can call you "Daddy" and you are not offended. I am your child! A child of the King! (Zechariah 9:9 and Romans 8:15-16).

You have prepared this day for me. Help me be aware of your presence and all the special blessings waiting for me—may I use them in your service. Guide me, hold me close so I may glorify you with each step I take.

Thank you for your love letter to me; I want to know me all the promises you made to me. I also want to know your instructions; may I understand them and learn to apply them to my daily living. I pray desperately that the Holy Spirit control my mind.

Fill me with joy and peace as I trust in you so that I may overflow with hope through your power. (Romans 15:13). Help me learn to be content in any situation, knowing my Abba is in control. (Philippians 4:12-13).

Since I belong to you, my cares and concerns are also yours. You can handle them; I can't. I love you, praise you and want to be of service to you.

Today in
Your Presence

— Day 1 —

Lord, it is in this very still, quietness that I can truly experience your presence. Other times I can know in my head you are with me; but in the stillness, I can know experientially your presence. During these early morning visits, there is an opportunity for my friendship with you to grow. You tell me you have loved me with an everlasting love and have drawn me to you with loving kindness. (Jeremiah 31:3). Thank you.

Thank you for your compassion that never fails. Your compassion is new each morning and your faithfulness is beyond measure. I see you each morning—and moment by moment—because my hope is in you. You are all I need. (Lamentations 3:22-26). Thank you for your Word.

You told Martha she could see a wonderful miracle if she believed; (John 11:40) and Lazarus came out of the grave. Lord, this is a season of miracles, and I believe you are the greatest of all miracles. You are omnipotent! You brought Lazarus back to life, and you yourself rose from the grave! I am asking you to bring the relationships in our family back to life. May each of us submit to you, your sovereignty, your will for our lives—and do as you tell us: love one another. Thank you. I know that is your will for us.

Let me just say "amen" to David's Psalm 28:1-3. What happiness when I have confessed my sin to you and been forgiven. What joys in this robe of righteousness! Thank you, Lord, for clearing my record.

Joshua 24:15 and prayers for each of my family. In your name, I am binding Satan from us. Love, honor, glory, thanksgiving go to you.

— *Day 2* —

Lord, thank you again this morning for allowing me to come into your presence for restoration. You are always with me and your Spirit lives within me, but this time is special.

Lord, you know my thoughts are often jumbled and disconnected; I hope they make sense to you. The Christmas season is a time of waiting, expecting, hoping, singing, and rejoicing. David says, "I will rejoice in the shadows of your wings." (Psalm 63:6-7). Yes, Lord, it is in the shelter and protection of your wings that I can rejoice and quietly wait in faith.

It is in my weakness(es) you have a stage on which to perform, to show your power. Lord, am I right, that you have never stop performing your miracles; am I just too blind to see them? I don't doubt you; I doubt me! I want my perspective to be the same as yours.

Like a kid who wants to open the presents early, I want to see your works, miracles, power today. However, faith allows me to be certain of things I cannot see. And, faith allows me to find abundant life as I quietly (sometimes not so quietly) wait.

You are faithful, loving, and constant. Thank you, Father, Lord, and Spirit—Father for sending, Son for coming, and Spirit for staying! Love, honor, praise go to you.

— *Day 3* —

Lord, day after day I continue to be amazed that you—Creator of heaven and earth—allow me to come to you, anytime, anyplace, anywhere with my jumbled thoughts and selfish desires. Thank you for that. I never want to take all that for granted. You created me so you know all about flaws, but you still welcome me. Thank you.

Lord, while I am here in your intimate presence, transform my thoughts to be your thoughts. I am a child of God; I want to be like my Father—to be like you. May your thoughts form in me (Isaiah 55:8-9) through your Spirit. May your Word speak to me in ways that I can hear your voice.

"Though I have not seen you, I love you; and even though I do not see you now, I believe in you. I am filled with an inexpressible and glorious joy, for I am receiving the goal of my faith, the salvation of my soul." (1 Peter 1:16-17). I simply come to you—but it is not a sacrifice for me, it is a joy. Here, I can tell you how grateful I am for all that you are—all that you have done and are doing for me. Thank you for this morning with you.

My decision is still Joshua 24:15. I ask you to bind Satan from me and my family that we may be a glory to you.

Love, praise, honor, and thanksgiving are yours.

— *Day 4* —

Lord, thank you for reminding me that I am not in this battle alone; when I call on your name, the battle becomes yours. Increase my faith and my trust as I allow you to fight for me. (Ephesians 6:10-18). Even Satan himself will bow before you. (Philippians 2:9-10). You are sovereign and omnipotent!

You know how to equip me so that I can stand firm; you are omniscient and omnipresent. Thank you, Lord, that you continue to help me. You have unlimited power to bless as well as protect. I am yours! Draw me closer and closer to you.

Lord, I am not certain whether I draw closer to you or you draw me closer to you. Either way, I want to be with you, trusting you completely. The devil and his underlings continue to be determined to interfere with our intimacy. I am resting in your promise that nothing can separate me from your love (Romans 8:38-39) and nothing can snatch me from your hand.

Lord, thank you for bringing to my attention that "I am receiving the goal of my faith—the salvation of my soul." (1 Peter 1:8-9). It is happening—not it will—it is in process. Let it continue because I love you and believe in you.

My decision is the same today; Joshua 24:15. That's my decision, but I need your strength and courage to follow through...to be faithful...to be steadfast.

Love, honor, praise go to you. What a glorious Lord you are! You daily bear my burdens and also give me my salvation. (Psalm 68:19).

— *Day 5* —

Over and over again, Lord, thank you for being here with me this a.m. Today, may your presence override everything else I experience. Train me to stay conscious of you in every situation I encounter. Help me remember your omnipresence and say to myself, "Surely the Lord is in this place." (Genesis 28:16).

And since this is true, that is my entrance into heaven! Lord, anytime I miss the major point of one of your truths in your Word, correct me; bring the truth to my attention. I am so limited; you are omniscient. I want to be aware of your presence, always!

Lord, you have more than met all my needs. David would say, "My cup runneth over." Teach me to open my heart to a hurting world. Through your prophet, Isaiah, you speak out against claiming to be religious and then neglecting the needs of those around me. (Isaiah 58:1-7).

Lord, I do want to love you wholeheartedly and my neighbor also. I am asking you to convict me of the hypocrisy in my life. Show me how I can have genuine worship that is active, hands on, and sacrificial— allowing your love to flow through me to those I encounter today and every day.

You told Martha that Mary had chosen what was important (Luke 10:42). Help me this day to choose what is important; having you in the forefront of my heart and mind. Purify my motives for the things I says yes to.

Joshua 24:15 is my choice today. Lord, just show me how "to do it right." Forgive me as you know I fail you often. You are omnipotent, Lord; bind Satan from me and each of my family.

May love, honor, praise, and thanksgiving go to you.

— *Day 6* —

Lord, this a chilly, rainy day and it is exactly as you planned it to be—a day to be spent close to you. Help me give you what you want most from me—my heart. I do want to love you with all my heart, soul, and strength (Deuteronomy 6:5) and yet I fail to do that. May your Spirit help me. Lord, never let my "religious activities" become a habit that gives me a false sense of security.

This time with you is precious! There is such joy and peace here in your presence. You created me to glorify you as well as enjoy you. May I always live close to you and allow you to guide me in and through the path you have for me. David would say "you fill me with joy in your presence and with eternal pleasures that are at your right hand." (Psalm 16:11).

Today, Lord, lead me to someone(s) who needs to experience your love and companionship. There let your love flow through me in your power—not mine. Use me to reach out to someone in need—to keep that heart from breaking.

Thank you for being all I need—even more. And, Lord, forgive me for sometimes searching elsewhere for satisfaction. May I seek you first this Christmas season and each day of the year.

Joshua 24:15...same decision again today. Same plea again today: "Bind Satan from me and each of my family." Thank you for doing that! Today may each of us glorify you.

Love, honor, praise, and thanksgiving belong to you.

— *Day 7* —

Lord, again this morning I thank you for your omnipotence—you are all powerful; for your omnipresence—you are always with me; for your omniscience—you are all knowing. But thank you most all for loving me...for loving each one of us. You are concerned with each detail of our lives, and nothing escapes your notice.

When I focus on you, I am safe and complete. It is when I let unresolved circumstances fill my consciousness that I become afraid. Help me remember you said I was worth more than a sparrow. (Matthew 10:29-31).

Teach me how to pray about every circumstance—to talk to you about every situation without telling you how to fix them or when to fix them. Lord, I want to learn to accept "today" as it is today. (Philippians 4:12). I want to learn what it is you want me to learn—that you love and care for me and will never leave me!!!

Lord, help me learn to wait in full confidence for you. Help me give you my impatience today and every day. May I rest in your love, and at the same time be your messenger. Show me—make me aware of—someone who could use encouragement or a helping hand.

Use me as Joshua 24:15 is still my decision this morning. (Moses left Egypt in spite of the king's anger. It was as though the king could see you with Moses. Lord, you haven't changed. Help me be aware of your presence with me and let others see you with me. (Hebrews 11:27).

Love, honor, praise, and thanksgiving belong to you.

— *Day 8* —

Lord, thank you for showing me who you are and for continuing to reveal more and more of your nature to me. I am a weak and needy person, and you just continue to meet my needs over and over again out of your glorious riches...just as you say you will. (Philippians 4:19). My needs and your riches are a perfect fit. I need a lot and you have unlimited supply.

Lord, never let me try to pacify my longings and insecurities with people, possessions, or power. You alone can fulfill my yearnings. And, you welcome me when I come to you with my defenses down asking you to make me whole.

Knowing your Word and your nature is my compass in any and every circumstance—especially when I don't feel your presence. It is then that I will sing your praises and trust you; you do not ignore my prayers when I call out for help. (Psalm 9:9-10).

Lord, you know there are times when I am in a spiritual wasteland—and it is a horrible place to be. It is there that I have to remember "What a God you are! You are perfect in every way! (Psalm 18:30). All your promises prove to be true! You are my shield! You never leave me!" (Joshua 1:5).

 Learning to walk in trusting obedience is not easy; it's hard. It is in difficult periods that I grow deeper in you, Lord. It is in these times I truly learn that you are omnipresent, omnipotent, and omniscient—and all loving to the end. Thank you for all that you are and all that you are to me. Joshua 24:15 is my decision again this morning.

Love, honor, praise and thanksgiving go to you.

— *Day 9* —

Lord, thank you again this morning for a TAG! More than once lately the phrase "God's Math" has hit my awareness; did you plan that?

I know you have a plan for me—for each one of us. When I seek you, I find all sorts of treasures in your Word that I love. Show me how to use these treasures in my life—how to love and serve. Help me get rid of my excuses. I don't have the gift of prophecy or hospitality; but I have the capacity to love you, Jesus, and—because of you—I can love others.

Yes, I am old, but I am yours! You tell me to test you just to see if you won't open the floodgates of heaven and pour out a blessing for me without measure. (Malachi 3:10). I have been in bible study most of my life—sometimes more deeply than others. I believe your Word is true and you keep every promise. Yes, you are faithful! You are abundant!

Lord, teach me all about "Gospel Math." I am greedy; I want every single blessing you have for me, and I want each one in full measure. Help me learn to follow you in obedience so I don't miss the blessing you have already prepared for me.

Just as you multiplied the five loaves and two fish to feed 5000 (Luke 9:13-17), when you do the math today there are blessings to go around for everyone. I just don't want to miss seeing all there is. I want to be obedient.

Joshua 24:15 is once again my decision. Oh, Lord, bind Satan. He continues to be out there roaming around, but you are omnipotent.

Love, honor, praise, as well as thanksgiving belong to you.

— *Day 10* —

Lord, you are faithful—always faithful—always keeping your promises. You never fail. You are my God. You strengthen me and help me day after day; you uphold me with your right hand. (Isaiah 41:10).

Lord, I am the problem even though I belong to you. I read and know your promises and then I assume you are going to fulfill those promises—exactly like *"I"* think they ought to be fulfilled—exactly like *"I"* want them to be at this moment. And when you don't do it my way, I begin to think you aren't going to come through this time. Forgive me, Lord. Give me faith to trust that you will do immeasurably more than I can even think to ask, all for your glory. (Ephesians 3:20).

Lord, even when I am faithless, you remain faithful and will help me. You always carry out your promises to me. (2 Timothy 2:13). Thank you.

Today help me keep you as the focal point of my security. I keep trying to make my life orderly and predictable; and in this world, that is not possible. Today let me be like David and just hold on to your powerful right hand (Psalm 139:10) for security and guidance.

Then James tells his Jewish Christian brothers to consider it pure joy to face trials. (1:2). I don't have trials of persecution like they faced. I am just selfish and want life easy, problem free, and my way. Forgive me, Lord. Help me see the radiance of your face and listen for your voice. Help me wait patiently, joyfully as you are keeping all your promises to me.

Joshua 24:15 continues to be my prayer and decision today. You deserve all my love, honor, praise and thanksgiving.

— *Day 11* —

Lord, thank you for continuing to expand your Word for me. I have read James 1:2-3 many, many times and it is marked in my Bible. In fact, my Bible just kind of opens to that page because I have gone there so often—You know all that. But, this morning you gave me something new as I read it. Thank you.

You tell me to "Consider it a great joy" when there are trials. You say "Then be happy; Consider it an opportunity for great joy; Consider it pure joy." You tell me to make a decision to be joyful. The circumstances are not altered! Nothing has changed! These poor Jewish Christians are still being persecuted, but they are to be joyful. The source of their joy—*YOU*—is still with them.

Lord, you are with me day after day! You never change! You are the source of my joy! When I am aware of your presence with me and open to your guidance, the channel is open for your joy to flow to me—for me to be changed—for me to grow in trust. Lord, I may not have said that exactly right; but my decision must be to focus on you—to be aware of your presence. You are the one who provides my joy.

In and of myself, I am not capable of being joyful in troubled times. I know you are with me and growing me in faith as I walk with you. I want not only to trust you and your Word but also to find joy in it as I go.

Joshua 24:15 is still my decision today. You know my concerns and I am leaving them with you. My love, honor, praise and thanksgiving go to you.

— *Day 12* —

Lord, this morning I come to you wanting to start this day new, fresh, desiring to be more like you today than ever before. Cleanse me and my heart; yes, wash me whiter than snow. You said to the thief beside you on the cross he would be with you in paradise. I want to be there with the two of you. I expect to see the woman at the well also. I have sinned just like they; cleanse me of all my sin and self-righteousness. It is only because of your grace that I have any hope of heaven.

I have access to grace: **G**od's **R**iches **A**t **C**hrist's **E**xpense.

You were in heaven with the Father. You set aside your deity, came to earth as a helpless baby to become a servant for the sole purpose of salvation: my salvation. If I had hung on the cross as you did, I would have thought "This is one thankless job!"

You lived a perfect life so that thought would never cross your mind. (Colossians 3:23-24). May anything/everything I do be for your glory, not mine. It is only because of the grace you provide that I am even here. Let me do everything without grumbling or complaining or arguing. (Philippians 2:14-15). Thank you for the grace you give.

May my attitude and my speech reflect the fruit of the Spirit who lives within me. May love, peace, joy, patience, kindness, goodness, faithfulness, gentleness, and self-control grow in me. (Galatians 5: 22-23).

My decision is Joshua 24:15. Strengthen me to live that out. All love and honor go to you.

— *Day 13* —

Lord, thank you for this holy time and it is holy—"set apart for sacred use." It is here in your presence that you are transforming me—recreating me to be more like you. Lord, I know that is a monumental job and it has taken miracle after miracle to get me this far. And you aren't through with me yet; I keep messing up your work. I will continue to set apart "this time" to seek your face.

It is here that I experience a nearness of you that strengthens my faith and fills me with peace. I don't say these things over and over for your benefit, Lord. I do it to remind me of all you are capable of. I want to live by faith—not sight. (2 Corinthians 5:7). I want to become a cleansed "temple of the Holy Spirit…" (1 Corinthians 6:19) "who is able to do immeasurably more than all I ask or imagine." (Ephesians 3:20). It is only through your power that any of that can happen.

Regardless of how often I fail you, I will continue to praise your name and ask you to forgive me. I will do as David did "speak of your glories and your grace. And when I am discouraged, I will seek your face and take heart. I will praise you." (Psalm 34:1-4).

I urgently ask for a special measure of courage and commitment for me and each of my family. Bind Satan from us all.

My thankfulness goes to you and well as my love.

— *Day 14* —

Lord, thank you for allowing me to come to you day after day—any day, any time—celebrating your birth and your resurrection. Your birth is good news and your resurrection is even better news.

I want to live in collaboration with you daily so my days will be meaningful. May I find and choose people to surround me that I can be open with on a spiritual level. May these people help me apply your Word to my life so that I may grow in you. Lord, may I gain wisdom.

You are the same yesterday and today and forever, (Hebrews 13:8), and that is so important. You never change. And I want to experience the reality of your presence each day. I want to acknowledge you in everything I do so you will have the opportunity to guide me to your plan or onto the path you have for me. (Proverbs 3:6).

Lord, help me be open to the wisdom you provide through your Word and to the insight your "chosen" offer. May they speak plain, hard truths into my personal life. May I live in such a way so as to reflect you, Lord. Help me remember my Christianity is not about "do's and don'ts" but my belief in you—about *YOU!*

Thank you for being with me through all the seasons of my life, especially the most difficult ones. And, no matter my circumstances, help me be open and willing for you to do your work in and through me.

Again my decision is Joshua 24:15. I am yours and I love, praise, and honor you. Thank you for your assurances in 1 Peter 5:6-7.

— *Day 15* —

Lord, I come this morning humbling myself under your mighty hand, asking forgiveness and strength to start fresh and new in you. You are here with me and you are always thinking about me and watching everything that concerns me. Thank you. Because of that I am leaving each—and all—of my worries and cares with you. (1 Peter 5:6-7). Lord, I do want to submit to you and your plan for my life—even at this late date.

May I always be full of your joy. May I always be unselfish and considerate so that others may see **you** and **your** works—not me and mine. Remind me to bring every situation and need to you in prayer and then leave everything in your care.

You have always provided for me; why do I even wonder that you might not in the future? Thank you for the peace that I experience when I am fully aware that you are here with me and leave everything in your care. (Philippians 4:4-7). Thank you for your Word and thank you that it is alive today just as it was for the church at Philippi.

Lord, you have always been gracious, kind and generous to me with your provisions for me—also with your protection of me. Thank you. Help me learn "the secret of contentment" in every situation. (Philippians 4:12). It is you who brings the peace and contentment; teach me.

My decision this morning is the same as yesterday: Joshua 24:15. I ask that you bind Satan from me and each of my family so that we may be a glory to you.

Love, honor, praise and thanksgiving be yours.

— *Day 16* —

Lord, write your words on my heart this morning as I am in your presence. May those around me see your letter in me; may I allow the Holy Spirit to have access to every part of me. May you be seen in all that I do and say. (2 Corinthians 3:2-3).

Lord, not only write on my heart, but speak to me in the depths of my being. I want to hear your voice. Never let me get so involved that am too busy to listen for you. Lord, awaken or open my ears to listen like one being taught. (Isaiah 50:4). Give me your words of wisdom; may I have your words to encourage those around me.

Your Spirit lives in me. You are love, peace, joy, patience, kindness, goodness, faithfulness, gentleness. Grow in me; give me self-control. (Galatians 5:22-23). Nail my evil desires to your cross. (...6:24). I want to live in your power and follow your lead in every area of my life (...6:25). You are all I need; it is your approval that counts.

Lord, I know who you are and what you have done; let this knowledge become wisdom. May I become more like you. May I overflow with hope to those around me. Use me, Lord.

Yes, it is my decision again this morning to love and serve you. (Joshua 24:15). Keep me free from Satan's touch.

All love, honor, praise and glory belong to you.

— *Day 17* —

Lord, I am seeking your face again this morning. "Let me not become weary in praying and give thanks as I watch for your answers." (Colossians 4:2). Lord, I am an empty shell without you—but you can fill me and make me complete. Today is a perfect day—but every day is—to come to you, depending on you with childlike trust.

I love the way you bring joy and peace to me when I rest quietly in your presence. I was amazed one day when I suddenly realized I no longer "felt alone." I could truly sing "Never Alone" (p. 400 of the old, old green Baptist Hymnal) and mean every word of it. Truly it is from you that all blessings flow.

Thank you for this Christmas season. I want to celebrate the fact that you set aside your throne in glory—with the Father in heaven—to reveal God to us. You came to draw us—me—to you, to cover my sins, to be my sacrifice, to show me how to live in love, to give me an abundant life. Thank you! What a wonderful Christmas present from you and our heavenly Father. It cost you so much; don't ever let me forget its value.

And, thank you for all the earthly blessings you allow me to enjoy as well. This family time is an extra special blessing!! May I use it to let your love flow through me to each one so our relationships will be more firmly established in you and for your glory.

Forgive me when I fail you. Even though I do fail you, my decision remains the same today: Joshua 24:15. Love, honor, praise, thanksgiving belong to you.

— *Day 18* —

Lord, you are omnipresent—with me right here—now. Thank you. You are omniscient, all knowing, and see the whole picture. I see only a small part of the picture. Thank you for being who you are. And, you are omnipotent; another **WOW**. Thank you. On these three premises, I should be at peace and relaxed. Lord, forgive me. I know these truths, and yet I still throw temper tantrums when I think you are taking too long to show up or when you don't work things out the "way I want you to."

And, while I am stomping my feet or whining, begging over and over for you to do it my way, I am missing out on the blessings you have for me now. My way may not be wrong; but your ways are better. (Isaiah 55:8-9). My way may be good for "one person," but your way is good for us all.

Lord, let me be like Peter (Luke 5:1-11) when he said, "I've given it my best shot and nothing is working. Now that I have listened to you, I will go do it differently because you said to. I will be obedient." I am awestruck by your power, mercy, grace, and love.

Lord, I want to be obedient. I will go deeper into your Word. I will draw closer to you. I will try to learn GPT—God's Perfect Timing— and let my obedience be based on your instruction.

Forgive me for failing you often, but my Joshua 24:15 decision still stands. Bind Satan—in **your** power, not mine—from me and each of my family.

All love, honor, and praise belong to you.

— *Day 19* —

Lord, I come this a.m. thankful for the earthly blessings you have given me—food, shelter, but most of all, a day with my two children! You are gracious! Yes, these things are temporary, but they are precious. And, as a child of the King—your child—I can only imagine how it pleases you when I come to you, really wanting to spend time with you.

And I can only imagine how you must feel when I go to your house—just because it is Sunday, and not because I am eager to come worshipping you or wanting to spend time at your house. Forgive me, Lord. Instill in me a deep desire to hear and obey your Word; may I joyously obey you; joyously go to your house, and joyously love your children.

Lord, show me how to get rid of any—all—of the clutter in my life that interferes with my goal of living close to you and being responsive to your leading. I want to hear you and I know you can communicate with me more readily if my mind is uncluttered and not focused on other things.

"May I seek first you kingdom and your righteousness and all these things will be given to me." (Matthew 6:33). Lord, bring order to my thoughts as I prioritize my life and activities according to your will. Let your presence infuse me with peace and joy. As I trust in you, may your peace and joy flow through me so others may have hope. (Romans 15:13).

Even though I don't get through a day without failures, my decision stands: Joshua 24:15.

Love, praise, glory, honor go to you. Thanksgiving goes to you as well.

— *Day 20* —

Lord, "submit and surrender" are words that normally mean defeat. Your Word tells me to trust you, lean on you, and in all my ways acknowledge you. (Proverbs 3:5-6). Here surrender tells me to leave the future to you, Lord.

I say I want to submit and surrender every area of my life to you. Then, I begin to ask myself what areas have I given fully, completely to you. Laughingly, Lord, I don't have a garage and am the only one in the bedroom, so I can easily say you can have those areas. I'm off to a good start. *:) :)*

Until I surrender all my relationships to you and forgive every slight or hurt, I will have stress.

Until I surrender my pocketbook to you, I will have financial stress. Everything belongs to you; have I followed your Word here?

Have I brought my secret sins to you, acknowledged them and agreed with you that they are sins? Have I asked for your forgiveness and for strength to "go and sin no more"? (John 8:11).

Lord, I want to fully submit/surrender every area to you. I want to hold up a white flag and surrender. I don't want to argue and fight with you about anything. I want the peace and joy I find when I agree with you. Let my faith and trust be expressed fully as I not just say "I surrender," but as I live in obedient submission to your Word.

I don't want to miss it!

Lord, at your birth your mama wrapped you in cloths and placed you in a manger, because there was no room at the inn. (Luke 2:17).

This Christmas season TV's, radios, websites, e-mails are bombarding me with the word, "holidays." I see beautifully decorated trees everywhere; and, of course, I have one. I see Santa's and elves, presents, tinsel, snow, mistletoe, parties. It's our cultural phenomenon: Christmas.

I can't miss Christmas! But, if I'm not careful, I can miss the very point of Christmas: celebrating your birth. That dilemma isn't new; it isn't just a product of today's society.

The innkeeper certainly missed the point of Christmas! His business was booming; rooms were full; he had work to do. He was so busy he didn't have time for a young, pregnant, peasant girl whose delivery date had arrived so he simply said "Sorry there's no room. I'm sold out."

Look what he missed! His marquee could have read "Son of God was born here." His inn could have had a permanent "Full occupancy" or "No vacancies" for the rest of his lifetime. He could have had the fame that wealth affords, but we don't even know his name. God came to earth in human form, and he could have played an unforgettable part in that drama, but he missed it because he was too busy.

Lord, I don't want to be so involved with Christmas activities that I don't have room for you. I want to celebrate your birth. You, Lord Jesus, must be first in my Christmas with my schedule, my plans, and my budget planned around you. I don't want to be like the innkeeper and miss the biggest opportunity of my life.

God, you are right here. You want to be a part of my life. And, getting to know you personally is an opportunity of a lifetime—***an opportunity I don't want to miss.***

More time with You on Day 20

Lord, I can come to the Throne of Grace all because of you and only through you. For that, I can rejoice. (1 Thessalonians 5:16-18). There is always something—some things—I can't control; in fact, there are very few things I can control, so I want to learn to pray constantly.

You have provided so many undeserved blessings, I must give you thanks. My most undeserved blessing is my salvation that cost you so much. Lord, no matter what else happens, may I just give thanks to you and walk closely with you.

You are the way, the truth, and the life and there is no other way but you. (John 14:6). You are the real thing. Satan is a great imitator and can even turn godly activities into counterfeit worship. Lord, I want to know you and your Word so intimately, thoroughly that I will easily be able to identify anything that is not from you and anyone who is not of you. May I see your face each morning before I see the face of another one of your children. (Matthew 6:33).

Lord, I am asking for absolution for not being the example for my children that I should have been. I can't change yesterday's years, but I am asking for guidance to love them as you would have them loved through me—in the time I have left. And, I am claiming my Romans 8:28 promise; you can work my failures out for your glory.

Lord, I recommit to my decision of Joshua 24:15. May I learn from you how to submit, obey, and serve you more perfectly. Bind Satan from me and each of my family.

Thanksgiving, love, praise, honor: all belong to you.

Another Holiday thought on Day 20

Lord, you know I've been in church as long as I can remember. Mom and Dad were faithful in teaching me about you day after day and year after year.

I've heard about Mary, Joseph, shepherds, angels, star, wise men, Herod and you over and over—notice I list you last.

When Herod asked the religious leaders what they knew about your birth, they answered him immediately that they did know: "Yes, he'll be born in Bethlehem in Judea." (Matthew 2:2-6). But, even though they knew the scriptures and had been in meetings with King Herod about your birth, the religious leaders weren't interested enough to go check out the birth of the new King. They wouldn't walk the five miles from Jerusalem to Bethlehem to see if the Messiah had truly come. Had they become bored with the religious rules and traditions?

Lord, I don't want to get locked into current traditions of decorating, gala affairs, presents, shopping, foods, Christmas cards, Santa Claus, and miss the Main Event—celebrating your birth and knowing the King.

Knowledge of you and traditions are great, but that's not why you came. You came so I could know all the characteristics of God and have a relationship with him. God, the Creator of the universe, wanted me to know him so He sent you to initiate the relationship and draw me to you.

That's the reason I celebrate. ***Thank you for coming!***

— *Day 21* —

Lord, thank you for your presence again this morning. I am amazed each day that the Creator of the universe would take time to be with me, have a dialogue with me, love me enough to pay a debt I couldn't pay, and love me now. I don't ever want to forget that! Today, Lord, I really want to hear your voice; may your Word speak to me.

A song keeps going through my head: Have Thine Own Way...Thou art the potter, I am the clay. Remind me that until you took me into your hands I was just a lumpy, messy, unattractive, cheap glob of clay. You give me value and purpose. When I go my own way and don't turn out the way you want, I have to be kneaded again—and again. You patiently start all over again. (Jeremiah 18:1-6).

Truly, Lord, I want to submit/surrender to your hands—the hands of the Potter. You know what you are doing. Continue to mold and make me into a vessel you can use for your purpose. May I be willing to let you do your work as it seems right to you.

I pray this and now I ask for your strength and comfort as you place me into the fire to be sealed and made ready for use. Help me be pliable, teachable, and sensitive to the work you want to do in my life. I want to become the person you want me to be. I want to be the "Pot," that piece of artwork, that others recognize and say, "Oh! That's a true Trinity piece of artwork."

Joshua 24:15 is still my prayer today, Lord.

— *Day 22* —

Lord, thank you for listening to me here in private—many times repeating myself. I believe you are Jesus Christ, my Lord and Savior. God raised you from the dead. Thank you for my salvation. (Romans 10:9-10). You never meant for me to take this journey of faith "alone" or "in secret." You gave me your Word—a wonderful, great and mighty gift that is just too precious to keep to myself.

Today I am asking you to infuse me with your power and strength to tell others and confirm my salvation. You are the Lord who generously answers my prayers and petitions. (Romans 10:11).

Lord, you know I cannot intellectually comprehend the how or even the why of your incarnation. I cannot understand why you would be willing to humble yourself to come and die for the likes of me, but I accept the fact that you did. Now, I ask you to help me be like the wise men, following the star, and falling down to truly worship you. (Matthew 2:10-11).

Lord, you deserve the praise and worship that comes as I wonder about all that you are and all that you have done for me. If I had a melodious voice, I would sing praises; instead I will enjoy your presence in silent adoration.

Your coming to earth is all because of your tender mercy and the tender mercy of our Father. (Luke 1:78-79). May your light lead me into the path of peace. May you give me strength and power to tell others the Good News.

My decision is Joshua 24:15; and my love, honor, praise, and thanksgiving belong to you.

Just another thought on Day 22

Lord, thank you for your obedience to our Father. Thank you for coming and dying on the cross to make peace between me and God. (2 Corinthians 5:18). My Father wants me to experience his favor and be reconciled to him—so He sent you.

Emotional peace is that peace with God. When my heart is broken, you give comforting peace. When I am confused, you give guiding peace. When I am ashamed, you give forgiving peace. You give peace for every problem or circumstance. Thank you, Lord.

When you died on the cross, you brought two opposing groups—Jews and Gentiles—together (Ephesians 2:14-16) into one body—yours. I want to bring every one of my relationships to you—under your power.

This Christmas and throughout the coming year may I rest in the most precious gift—your peace. Your peace unites me with God our Father, with my inner self, and with others.

Thank you for a peaceful Christmas.

— *Day 23* —

Lord, long before you came as the perfect gift to us and a sacrifice for us, our Father was promising good gifts: e.g. for Abraham, land; Joshua, your presence and land; seven times God, the Father, told Joshua "I have given you this land." The land was rightfully theirs, a gift from God. They **only** had to claim it and that wasn't easy.

Lord, I want to claim every gift you have for me. The most important gift is your presence. You promised never to abandon or fail to help Joshua. (Joshua 1:5). I am claiming that promise for myself. You told Joshua to be strong and courageous (v. 6); only as you sustain me can I do that, Lord.

You desire that I "take up my cross daily" and follow you; give me the courage to do that. Truly I need the courage that only you can give to step out in faith—especially in scary situations.

I am like the Israelites; you have given me gifts, treasures, and blessings that I haven't claimed. Your Word tells me (Ephesians 1:3) that you have "blessed me with every blessing in heaven because I belong to you." **WOW!** You have good gifts waiting for me if I will be obedient—using the strength and courage you provide—to claim them. They are my inheritance.

All I can say is "Lord, thank you for your goodness and generosity to me. Help me—I'm back to my basic plea 'help me'—be courageous and obedient so I can possess all the gifts you have already tagged as "Merry Christmas! For: Lee. With love, from: God, your heavenly Father."

My decision this a.m. is Joshua 24:15. I need your name and power to bind Satan from me and each of my family.

Love, honor, and praise go to you.

— Day 24 —

Lord, truly, it is "Joy to the World" today. What Joy came to the world through your birth—and when you completed your earthy mission, your resurrection!

Mary, your mother, is one of my favorite people in your Word. What faith! She couldn't haven't have been more than an innocent 13-year-old girl when the angel told her she would be the mother of God. She simply responds with "I am yours and I'll do what you want me to." (Luke 2:38).

Oh! What faith! She knew she could be stoned for having a child out of wedlock. She knew her finance could choose to reject her! And, still she said, "I am willing." What an honor to be the "mother of God."

But, not all the true blessings come without pain and suffering. You, Lord, experienced the pain of the nails as they were driven into you and as you hung on the cross. Apparently, Mary accepted God's plan for her life and was faithful to the end as she witnessed her son's torturous death. Lord, I want to be like that—graciously accepting your will for me.

Lord, you know me. More often, I am more like Job "complaining, restless, anxious." (Job 3:25-26). Lord, I want to remember that whatever you give is given in love and that you remain sovereign.

In the midst of her pain, as Mary saw you hanging on the cross, she may not have at that moment thought "What an act of love! This is a blessing and I am thankful." But, truly it was the greatest of all acts of love. May I respond in faithful obedience.

Your love comes in a variety of gifts. Some involve pain and suffering. Even if they do, help me surrender as Mary did, saying "I am yours, and may I accept your will for me life." (Luke 17:5-10).

— *Day 25* —

Lord, the miracle of any birth is breath-taking, but the miracle of your birth is beyond awesome. "The Word became flesh and dwelt among us." (John 1:14).

To think you would give up the glory of heaven and accept the limitations of infancy in appalling, filthy conditions of a stable just so I—we— could know the length and depth of your love and God's love is beyond comprehension.

To think you knew ahead of time all you would suffer and you still came down to earth so I—we—could go up to heaven; yes, a miracle. (Philippians 2:6-7). No wonder the angels sang "Glory to God in the highest." (Luke 2:13-14). You were rich and became poor; and, when I believe in you as the Son of God, I have access to all the riches of your throne. (2 Corinthians 8:9). ***WOW!***

Lord, as I sit here with you this morning, I want to be fully aware of the light your birth brought to a dark world. May your light shine into my heart so I more fully understand and utilize the knowledge of you—to glorify you.

You came and lived in my world; you understand—God understands! You understand and still engage in my life. I see you in fogs and sunrises, laughter in winds that rustle the leaves, friendships that continue over the years as well as all of life's events: even in sadness and loss of a spouse.

Thank you for coming and thank you for not stopping before you conquered death. You give hope. All love, praise, and honor belong to you.

— *Day 26* —

Lord, thank you for being here with me now in these "wee hours" (2:00 a.m.) for reminding me that your love does not depend on my circumstances or happenings around me.

As I read Psalm 27:4, I say it just as David said it. "The one thing I want from you, the thing I seek most of all is the privilege of meditating here in your presence, living in your presence every day of my life, delighting in your incomparable perfections and glory." You humbled yourself and took my sin to the cross. You cared that much about me; you care about me now.

If I truly seek your presence first, I will know that I can bring all my cares to you. If I am in your perfections, I will know your peace. If your glorification is my chief desire, I will remember you are omnipotent, omniscient, omnipresent and rest. Instead of saying I want one thing from you, I am asking you to quiet my heart and mind, Lord, so that I have only one request—to know you and dwell intimately with you.

It is wonderful that I can bring each and every concern I have to you, but I don't want to become so focused on my prayer list that I forget about the love relationship that I am privileged to have with you. "My spirits may droop, yet you are constant. You are my strength. I am yours forever." (Psalm 73:26). "I want to get as close as I can to you, and I will tell others about the wonderful ways you care for me." (Psalm 73:28).

Lord, I want to be satisfied with you alone and realize that when I have you, I have everything I could possibly need. (Matthew 6:33).

Continued on page 182...

...Continued from page 181

I have no reason to fear because I am in you; I am confident you will keep me close to you. I pray that you will reveal yourself to those close to me so they will have that same confidence in you that I have and know your peace. Let them know that your love for them does not depend on their circumstances. Give each of them a desire to know you more intimately.

Lord, you ask us to "Come and talk with you." (Psalm 27:8). Give each of us a desire to be close to you. May each of us seek your face and listen for your voice and follow your guidance.

I want to be patient. (27:14). I am waiting and I thank you for the miracles you are performing now—at whatever stage they are. Yes, I am waiting as you tell me to. I am giving you my permission to divinely interfere in our lives as you see fit. "As far as me and my family, we will serve you." (Joshua 24:15). I love you, praise you and thank you.

Never Alone

Lord, thank you for your presence with me during the night and still again this morning. You are forever faithful. Thank you for allowing me to bring my concerns to you at any moment. Help me focus on **real** problems and give me spiritual energy to respond with godly solutions.

Lord, my decision is Joshua 24:15 and today I lift up each one of my family to you for their growth toward you. It is in your name—your omnipotence—that I ask you to bind Satan from them, and I thank you for the miracles you are performing at this moment. Draw us close to you and restore our relationships so we may be revived and rejoice in you. (Psalm 85:6).

It is in you—when I am totally open with you—when I agree with you about what sin is and ask for forgiveness—that I find mercy and peace. (Proverbs 28:13). May I walk contritely with you today. (Psalm 51:17).

Lord, I know you don't have grandchildren; each of us is your child. I can't make decisions for my family, but I still pray Joshua 24:15 today. I love you, Lord! I praise you! May I honor you in all that I do and say! I will not worry (Matthew 6:25); I am yours!

And I know your eyes are on my family and we don't have to walk alone.

— *Day 27* —

Lord, just as the weather changed from 3 degrees last week to a summer 77 degrees yesterday, circumstances fluctuate all the time; but you remain steadfast, faithful, and never changing. Thank you. Lord, I want to be faithful to you! I want to be faithful during a season of testing so that it may be a season of growth.

"From you and through you and to you are all things. To you be the glory forever. Amen." (Romans 11:36). Help me remember that I don't have to wait until the trial has ended to see your glory; your glory is in the trial as well. Lord, your glory was in the fiery furnace waiting for the three men as they entered the heat. You were there with them and for them—all the way. (Daniel 3:16-26).

Lord, you are not a silent God. Help me hear the truths in your Word and make my decisions based on them. May I find your glory—see it—in and through even the mundane and hurtful parts of life. Your glory abounds daily! It never fails or changes—regardless of circumstance or mood.

Lord, as I move through situations that seem to go on forever, your glory is not waiting to be revealed at some later date. It is revealed as I am obedient to you day after day—each day. Help me choose to live my life this day in a way that reveals your constant presence and glory.

I saw your glory revealed one night years ago at a hospital in OKC. Dick and LaTayne were praying and singing quietly in the waiting room when they were told their son, Benji, had died from injuries he received in a car accident. Their praises did not waiver as they absorbed the news of their loss; your glory was evident.

Today, help me see your glory and identify your goodness and grace in your creation; in acts of kindness all around me. May others see it in me as I focus on you and allow your love to flow through me.

— *Day 28* —

Lord, as I start this day, let me just repeat David: "You are my strength and my refuge, an ever-present help in times of trouble." (Psalm 46:1-3). Help me write that on my heart and the back of my eyelids so I am constantly aware of your presence and need not be afraid of anything—even circumstances of epidemic proportions.

When I am fearful, I fail to see you in the midst of the situation. Each day your grace and glory are in countless places all around me; open my eyes to see them and my heart to acknowledge them. May I proclaim your abiding presence as I go through this day.

Thank you, Lord, for the gift you give—peace of mind and heart! There is strength and stamina in the peace you give; I don't need to be afraid. (John 14:27).

You also give me identity; I am a child of the King. That identity is secure; it can't be hacked or duplicated. I am yours; and I can always count on you—a powerful, sovereign God who pours out your blessings on me. You are ***Jehovah-jireh!***

You provide whatever I need to boldly face any challenge or situation. You care about everything that touches my life. You are a loving, compassionate listener—even when I repeat myself so often. Thank you for this access to you, to my heavenly Father, and to his storehouse of riches—my inheritance.

Ask: I ask for wisdom. Seek: I seek your faithfulness. Knock: I knock to have the door opened to discover all the goodness of you. Again, I am yours; and without you, I am nothing. No one compares to you. Today may I have the opportunity and courage to share this with someone who needs your touch.

Joshua 24:15 is my prayer. Love, honor, thanksgiving to you.

— *Day 29* —

Lord, thank you for your presence with me now. I want to confess every sin to you now so when I see you Face to face I won't have anything hidden to be ashamed of. I know nothing is ever really hidden from you. From this day forward, my hope is I will never do anything that will cause me to be ashamed of myself, that I will be ready to speak out boldly for you, and that I will be an honor to you. (Philippians 1:20).

May I grow so that I trust you with every fiber of my being; without you, I can do nothing of value. May I learn to trust you in both good and bad times; I just want my trust to be constant. (Psalm 40:4; 56:3-4; 62:8). Lord, I truly like the peace that comes when I am focused on you—my Rock and my Refuge. (Isaiah 26:3-4). You are eternal!

Lord, I want to know your Word so I have a true plumb line, a guide, a light! I live in this world, but I want to live by your standard. (2 Corinthians 12:10). I want to learn to put others first. (Matthew 20:16). Lord, choose me to be rich in faith (James 2:5) and teach me true humility. (Matthew 5:5).

Forgive me, Lord. When I have longed for the "happily ever after," remind me that's what eternity with you, the Father, and heaven is. Help me reject discontent and complaining. May I never try to substitute a person, place, or thing for you in my heart. May your Word speak clarity to my expectations.

Lord, I choose to serve you today. Love, honor, praise, and thanksgiving are due you.

— *Day 30* —

Lord, you have spoken to me time and time again, but often I haven't listened. You have called me, but I didn't answer. (Jeremiah 7:13). Forgive me, Lord; forgive me.

I am always in your presence and you are continuously calling. I may even be listening as you begin the conversation; but I let other, insignificant distractions become my focus—and miss out on valuable time with you. You want to share every part of yourself with me.

Lord, don't give up on me; help me unplug from the world and become focused on you. I want to hear your voice and your life-giving instructions. Lord, I don't want to just go through religious motions. I don't want to be like your people were when you sent Jeremiah to call them back to you. I want my heart to be fully in tune with you and my ears listening for your voice. I need your guidance and instructions.

Adultery and murder aren't my sins, but I have let other things and people come between us. And sin is sin. Forgive me of this "idol worship"; I want no false gods in my house. I want to be transformed by you each day as I come to you so I can experience your blessings over and over. I want to sense your power and your presence as I approach your throne—the Throne of Grace—with open ears and an attentive heart.

My decision is new this morning, "As for me and my family, we will serve you." (Joshua 24:15). I do love you, Lord. You have my praise and thanksgiving, and I ask you to bind Satan from each of us this day.

— *Day 31* —

Lord, as I sit here with you this last day of the year, I thank you again for your presence and the peace you provide—the peace that only you can give.

I can rest because I have seen how you have provided for me so faithfully throughout this year and all my 80+ years. I like the idea that your abundance and my neediness are a perfect match. You created me with a hole in my heart that only you can fill. Without you, I am a cripple; but in you, I am healed and whole.

Lord, it is your all-surpassing power within me (2 Corinthians 4:7) that continues to heal me. It is your tender loving mercy that grows me toward you and in you. (Ephesians 4:15-16). It is your grace that compels me to desire to be more like you. (Titus 2:12). It is your love that I want to submit to. You died so I could live. (2 Corinthians 5:14-15).

Lord, I want to grow up; I don't want to always be a spoiled brat. (Ephesians 4:14). It is only when I am intimate with you and the Father that I can mature. I want to have the kind of fruit that the Holy Spirit produces: love, joy, peace, patience, kindness, goodness, faithfulness, gentleness, and self-control. (Galatians 5:22-23).

Lord, you promise "to teach me all things and remind me of all your promises;" help me be open to your instructions. Let your love flow through me as I trust you. I have made my Joshua 24:15 decision and I need you to bind Satan from me and my house. Yes, Lord, I love, praise, honor, and give you thanks.

Can't Thank You Enough, Lord

— *Day 1* —

Lord, thank you for letting us come to you for a fresh start—any moment, day, month, or year. Together we start another season—you and I.

I come to you, eager to be changed. I am bringing you a teachable spirit. I want to be transformed by renewing my mind each morning in you. (Romans 12:2). I want to walk with you knowing what God's good, pleasing, and perfect will is. Let my mind be open to you, may my eyes see you, my ears hear you, and my heart respond to your life-changing love.

Thank you for creating me and allowing me to grow up in a home where you were honored. Thank you for the salvation you provide and your continued presence year after year. You know me and understand me completely and you continue to amaze me with your constant embrace of everlasting love. Even at this late stage of my life you have "plans for me;" and they are "plans to prosper me and not plans to harm me, plans to give me hope and a future." (Jeremiah 29:11).

Lord, I want to start this year's adventure fully aware of your presence. I want to become more attentive to your leading. I want to see you in every situation; I want to hear your voice. My New Year's resolution is "I will search for you and for your strength, and just keep on searching." (Psalm 105:4).

I love you and my Joshua 24:15 decision is the same today as it has been. Bind Satan from me and each of my family this day.

Love, honor, praise, and thanksgiving belong to you.

— *Day 2* —

Lord, today I am so thankful that you meet with me in the early morning. I love my TAG! Today I asking you to help me understand/know what you want me to do at this late stage of my life and asking you to make me wise in you. I want to live in a way that pleases you and honors you. I want to be doing good, kind things for others and at the same time getting to know you better and better. (Colossians 1:9-10).

I am asking you to fill me with your glorious, mighty strength so I can keep going no matter what happens—always full of your joy. (Colossians 1:11). I want to be like David when he learned of his baby son's death; he got up, bathed, went to the temple and worshipped. (2 Samuel 12:16-23). Lord, I want to be able to accept any circumstance with thanksgiving, worshiping you. I want to always rely on your faithfulness and live in gratitude in every situation, despite the outcome.

Paul says in Philippians 4:12 that he had learned the secret of contentment regardless of the circumstance and he is in prison as he says that. He could only say that because you were in him and with him. I want to learn that secret also.

Lord, I have told you the things I want from you this morning. Again I am "I centered." I first tell you what I want and ask you to cleanse me before I begin any praise or thanksgiving. It is here in humility I ask to be transformed to be like you.

My Joshua 24:15 decision has not changed. Love, honor, praise, thanksgiving all go to you.

— *Day 3* —

Lord, I have to thank you first for being here with me; the very fact that you meet with me each morning never ceases to amaze me. The God of the universe, Creator of the world, King of kings, Lord of lords here with me! **WOW!** Thank you just isn't enough. (Psalm 105:4).

I am nothing without you so I come in repentance for allowing "people, things, circumstances" to take your place in my heart. I offer my prayers with fervency and persistence. I ask for refreshment and renewal as I allow the Light of your presence to soak into every part of my being. This time with you is not a sacrifice but a necessity for my survival; it strengthens me for the day. Thank you for reminding me that I "have chosen what is better and it will not be taken from me. (Luke 10:39-42).

"How great is your goodness." Thank you for hiding me in the secret place of your presence as I take refuge in your peace. (Psalm 31:19-20). I can enjoy your shelter. I know of no one person who is attacking me —thank you; but the Devil himself is attacking my family. Help us all and let Satan be bound by and through the power of your name.

Thank you for the peace and confidence I find in you alone. You tell me to expect trials, distress, and frustration. And, you tell me to be of good cheer—take courage, be confident, be undaunted, be certain—because you have overcome the world. (John 16:33). You have deprived Satan of his ability to harm me; you have bound him this day for me. Thank you.

May my faith hold onto your promises for me and each of my family as we serve you. (Nehemiah 1:4-7).

— *Day 4* —

Lord, I can think of no better way to start this a.m. with you than to **remember** you are the omnipotent, omniscient, omnipresent Son of God who humbly left the throne of grace and came to earth to die for my sins on a cruel cross—and **give thanks**. Then you rose from the grave, later ascended into heaven and now reign forever with the Father. Lord, grow my trust and faith in all that that means.

Thank you for your Word that teaches me how to live out my faith being obedient to you. I want to "automatically" say, "I trust you, Jesus" in response to any and every event of my life. I want to think about who you are, all your power and glory, and your love for me. Then, help me, Lord, to be Daniel who obediently proclaimed his faith in you even as he faced execution in the lion's den.

You are sovereign over—and in—every situation in the universe. You were in the lion's den and closed their mouths. I can only imagine how Daniel's confidence in you grew each time he was obedient and saw you at work. You are the same faithful God today as you were then.

You didn't take away any adverse conditions that Daniel experienced. You were simply with him when he slept and you gave him answers for the king's dreams. You heard him as he opened the windows three times a day and prayed. You were with him when he wrote on the wall as you gave your message. You are still that same faithful God—the Trinity. I want to know your power and glory and then be obedient to you. Joshua 24:15 is my decision once again.

Love, honor, praise, and thanksgiving go to you.

— *Day 5* —

Lord, I thank you for my weaknesses and for each failure, because they have taught me to rely on you. Truly without you, I am nothing. Apart from you I am wasted.

This morning I come to you with an open mind and heart asking you to place your desires in me. Yes, I continue to ask you to bless the things I have decided to do; but, Lord, keep me be so close to you that I only want to do what pleases you. When there is something that you want me to do and I know I cannot do it alone, call me and clearly remind me to depend on you—reassuring me of your presence with me.

I want to continue my faith-walk with you; I want to learn to lean on you with each step I take. It is only when I depend on you that my faith grows. I want to see your miracles. You are the same God today as you were with Joshua, Daniel, David, et al. You are still the God of miracles; I want to see them.

Yes, Lord, you are great and awesome and you keep your every promise. You are loving and kind. You are merciful when I come to you acknowledging that I have sinned against you. Continue to reveal my sin(s) to me so I can come to you on bended knees asking for forgiveness. I want to be near you; my soul searches for you; my whole body longs for you—just as David's did. (Psalm 63:1-2).

Thank you for the miracles you are working at this moment. Help me see them. Hear my cries for you to bind Satan from me and my family so we may truly live out Joshua 24:15.

Love, honor, praise, and thanksgiving go to you.

— Day 6 —

Lord, you are kind and merciful, slow to anger, and full of love and compassion for us all. And, today I thank you for being all that. And, as I go about my day, I will bless your name, talk about your glory, and tell of your miracles. You lift me up when I am downcast; you continue to provide for me; you are kind and answer when I humbly call on you. You never leave me alone. Your protection is all around me. I will praise you this day. (Psalm 145:8-21).

Lord, you are able to do far more than I can ask or even imagine. (Ephesians 3:20-21). Knowing there is no limit to your power and knowing you do not withhold good from me as I live close to you, (Psalm 84:11), I lay every care at your feet this morning. I won't even list them; I'm just dumping them. They are yours now.

Lord, I am asking you to control my mind because there is life and peace in you. (Romans 8:6). I will not be discouraged because some of my prayers are not yet answered and some of the situations remain unchanged. Wait! Wait! Wait! Time teaches me to trust you more firmly and grow stronger. (Isaiah 40:30-31).

Lord, I know there isn't a "miracle" without a "problem" at its base. The scene is set and I am waiting for you to perform your divine intervention in all your power and glory. I am keeping my eyes, ears, and mind open—waiting to applaud you and all that you are doing.

Let your first miracle continue in my heart. You died on the cross to save me, but you are NOT through with me yet. My decision is still Joshua 24:15 and my love, honor, praise and thanksgiving go to you.

— *Day 7* —

Lord, it is impossible to praise you too much—to thank you too often—to love you too much. You deserve all I have to give and more! May my adoration be a continuous overflow of joy—the joy that comes from your presence with me. David says, "You inhabit our praise." (Psalm 22:3).

Lord, I want to praise, thank, and love you in every situation—even when the situation is not as I would have it—even when my outpouring is more disciplined than spontaneous! "Praise you, Lord! Praise you, Lord! I will praise you all of my life; I will sing praises to you and to my Father in heaven as long as I live." (Psalm 146:1-2). And, I will — with your help— learn to "give thanks in all circumstances, for I know that is what you want from me since I am in you." (1 Thessalonians 5:18). Without you, I am nothing; and without you, anything I have is worthless trash.

Lord, it is you that fills the empty hole in my heart. It is you who takes away my loneliness. It is your love and compassion that gives strength. Thank you for your Word and I ask you to grow my hunger for it. May I find and claim every promise you have for me.

Thank you for the community where I live. Thank you for the Christian heritage you gave me as a child that I saw modeled in my home. I ask forgiveness because I failed you so often as a wife and parent...and as your child.

My decision today is Joshua 24:15 and I ask you to take my failures and make them into something beautiful. Draw each of us closer and closer to you.

Love, honor, praise, thanksgiving go to you and I surrender in obedience to you.

— *Day 8* —

Lord, today I want to start with Joshua 24:15—where I usually end. Thank you for the foundation you gave me through the loving care of Christian parents. They probably prayed that same verse over and over as they reared us; and they may have felt the same sense of failure I feel when each of us went our separate ways. Thank you that they just quietly surrendered to you in obedience.

Today, "As for as me and my house, we will serve you" is my prayer. As each of my children, their spouses and their children are on separate life paths, I pray they will never lose sight of you, never stop listening for your voice, and always ask for your guidance. Lord, you know I want them to know you fully.

Life is full of unpleasant circumstances, bad decisions, and painful consequences. May each of us bring them to the foot of the cross and find redemption in you. In you, hope is restored. In you and your grace, we can find healing for our brokenness. May each of us remember that's why you came—to save each of us from our brokenness.

Thank you for not holding my sin against me! May I be willing to "submit/surrender" in full obedience to you. Lord, I am learning it is harder for me to trust you to meet my family's needs than it is for me to trust you to meet my own needs. Why? Am I that egotistical? Help me remember you love each of my family more than I do. They have needs I can't fix and problems I can't solve. What else can I do but trust you!

And trust comes like manna. I can't store it up, but I can receive it fresh and new each day. That is enough. Thank you for your sufficiency. I love you, Lord.

— Day 9 —

I thank you for who you are and for sharing your early morning hours with me. Lord, it is in you that I find rest, strength, and a way to the Throne of Grace. It is you who gives me perseverance and endurance so I can be a witness for my Father. It is you who bought my salvation. (Psalm 62:1). Yes, you alone are my Rock, my Rescuer, defense and fortress (62:2)—even as I fail you. Forgive my failures.

Lord, you are more than enough. You are everything I need. I pray that I will never let some circumstance, possession, or person determine my happiness or interrupt my connection to you. I want no idol before me.

Help me run to you, especially in times of trouble. I want to approach the Throne of Grace in confidence—knowing I will find mercy and help. (Hebrews 4:16). When I come to the Throne, I pray my motives will be in tune with you. (James 4:3). And I want to rest on your Word that as I desperately cry out to you, you hear me. (Psalm 55:17).

Grow my trust and confidence in you, Lord. The truth of your Word stands today. You haven't changed; you are faithful; you keep your promises. You are my ever-present Helper and you are omnipotent. (Romans 8:31). Nothing is impossible with you. (Luke 1:37). You are all I need; you are sufficient. (Psalm 46:1-3).

Lord, teach me GPT—God's Perfect Time. Today I want to walk with you, at your pace and aware of your presence, enjoying each step.

Joshua 24:15 is my commitment.

— Day 10 —

This morning, I start with "Thank you for _____." Fill in the blank. If I have "it," "it" is a gift from you. It doesn't matter if it is the bed I sleep in, money in the bank, or life itself; it is a gift from your bounty. If it is a circumstance I don't like, it still has your permission or it wouldn't be there. May I learn to say "Thank you" here also. Here is where I am asking you to teach me—grow me.

I want to grow in trust and faith. Each time I reaffirm my trust in you, I am growing and making preparation for days ahead. Even though my steps of faith and trust may be terribly small, the more I trust you— the more you empower me.

David said (Psalm 56:3-4) "When I am afraid, I will trust in you" and then repeated himself, ending with "What can mortal man do to me?" Thank you for giving me security beyond this life; no one can rob me of my promise of eternity with you.

Today when not much is happening in my world, I want to "practice trusting" you. Show me how to "store up treasures in heaven." (Matthew 6:20-21). I don't want to just sit here and talk about "trust and faith;" I want to trust you with my whole being and take that step "out of the boat" as Peter did. Empower me, Lord.

But, until then, I will again echo David—the man after God's own heart. "Wait for the Lord; be strong and courageous. Wait for the Lord." Psalm 27:14). Lord, I will wait for you. I screw things up when I run ahead on my own—ahead of you.

My decision this morning is the same: Joshua 24:15. My love, honor, praise, and thanksgiving go to you.

— *Day 11* —

Lord, your Word tells me to "wait for you; to be strong and courageous... to wait for you." (Psalm 27:14). You are here with me this morning, and I say you are sufficient—all I need. Yet, I wait for some circumstance to change.

Lord, help me focus not on the "wait" but on the "be strong and courageous." In the face of heartache, disappointment, tension, and fear—help me realize you desire my growth in strength and courage as I wait hoping for things to change. You desire growth in my strength and courage as I wait—but you also desire that I lean on, depend on, seek you now, today!

Lord, I will always be waiting for something. As I wait, I want to remember your promise to be with me always. (Joshua 1:5). I can be confident in your presence and in your omniscience. You have knowledge of things ahead that I cannot see. Help me just stay focused on you in the present; I don't want to miss the "now" as I keep looking ahead for the "future". You, yourself said, "My Father is always working and I am working also." (Joshua 5:17).

Lord, I can't remember what interrupted me at this point, and now other things must be taken care of. Help me be aware of you throughout the rest of this day.

— *Day 12* —

Thank you, Lord, for always being available to me as a source of strength and guidance. When I go elsewhere—self-help books, other people's opinions, current periodicals—I can come up empty handed. It is only you who gives me the answers and strength I need. The answers are in your Word! I haven't always gotten it right, but you are faithful.

Again, still, I need you. After I get the information from your Word that I need, have the knowledge, I need your wisdom to apply your Word to the situation—as you want me to. You don't change, Solomon asked for wisdom, (2 Chronicles 1:10) and you granted it. Grant me wisdom also, Lord! Also, grant me the desire to please you and to follow your instruction.

"Reverence and fear of God are basic to all wisdom. Knowing God results in every kind of understanding." (Proverbs 9:10). And, it is through you, Lord, that I can know the Father. I want to know the Truth and have faith to apply wisdom in my actions.

Today, may I speak kind words where there is conflict. May I shower love and patience on each person I encounter. May I simply hold each person I meet today up to you and remember he or she is your child just as I am.

Here I am again, Lord, back to my standard, fall-back prayer: "Thank you. Help me." All I know with absolute certainty is I love you and need you.

My decision remains: Joshua 24:15. My love, praise, and thanksgiving go to you.

— *Day 13* —

Lord, thank you for your faithfulness. I am constantly amazed at the extraordinary measures you take to draw your children—including me—to you. For thousands of generations you have kept your promises to those who love you and keep your commands. (Deuteronomy 7:9). You are not slow to fulfill your promises; your timing is perfect; you are patient so that none would perish. (2 Peter 3:9). And, you wait patiently for us who believe in you, to tell others the good news of your coming—the first and the second coming.

I know I can come to you with my "weaknesses"; I can ask anything that is according to your will (James 4:3), and I know you hear me. (Isaiah 59:1). I want to trust you totally; I don't want to be like the Israelites who didn't get into the Promised Land because they failed to trust you. (Hebrews 3:19).

Lord, help me release my concerns to you; you know all about them. Help me fix my eyes on you and see your will for this situation; I am not capable to changing anything or knowing what to change. Open my eyes to see your hand in every detail of my life and those around me. May I come to you in this precious, intimate time in total surrender.

The devil himself is out there and will try to get me to "pick up/take back" the cares I've just given you. (1 Peter 5:7-8). You are "OOOO" —omnipotent, omniscient, omnipresent, and the Omega; and I am in your protection/your loving arms. My cares are secure in you. You and the Father are one, and my heavenly Father is bigger than...greater than...

This is the day you have made; I will rejoice in it and in you. My decision is Joshua 24:15; even so, I ask forgiveness because I fail you so often.

I love, honor, praise and give thanks to you.

— *Day 14* —

Lord, as we are here together this morning, I continue to ask you to fill me with your fruit—your grace. May my mind and heart be open to receive all you have for me. You know every part of my being; you created me. You know my needs and you alone can meet them. There is no room for pretense in my relationship with you; you see straight through me and into my heart.

I know nothing can separate me from your love (Romans 8:38-39), but I am such a "wimp." I have failed you in every stage of my life; I don't see how you can continue to love me, but you do. Lord, in this final stage of my life, I am asking you to transform my weaknesses into strengths—not for my glory or satisfaction, but YOURS. Use me.

You didn't come for my comfort; you came to save me and to continue making me into your image. Lord, continue to reproduce your character in me. (Ephesians 4:22-24).

Lord, every time I try to control my circumstances, my future, the people around me, I am trying to be God; forgive me. Just teach me your values, your attitudes, and your character so I can be godly. I want to be Christlike. (Matthew 5:1-12; Galatians 5:22-23; 1 Corinthians 13; 2 Peter 1: 5-8).

May I just rely on you—still serve and praise you. Joshua 24:15. May my love, honor, praise, and thanks be yours.

— *Day 15* —

Lord, in you there is Peace beyond understanding. There are circumstances that remain unchanged: the loss of loved ones, broken relationships, prodigals that haven't yet returned. You know all that. Yes, the wind and the waves are there: and without you, I would sink. (Matthew 14:29-30).

Here in my TAG, I am safe and secure. I am Face to face with you. I can focus—fix my eyes—on you who never changes. (Hebrews 12:2). I can thank you for all that you are, for all you have done and are in the process of doing, and ask the same thing of you that Peter asked, "Lord, save me." (Matthew 14:31). Yes, help me too, Lord. Help me step out of the boat and be the minister you want me to be. You are always beside me, helping me face today's wind and waves. May I keep my focus on you.

Give me a touch of your grace that meets every need. Allow me to give comfort and encouragement to those who are hurting because someone they love doesn't love you; because a child is living a dangerous lifestyle; and just because they have other hurts in their lives. They are your children; help me touch them. May I see their need through your eyes; and through your strength and grace, lift them up.

You have been so gracious to me, Lord; and I am certain of this: You are with me always—today and tomorrow—even to the end of the world. (Matthew 28:20). Use me.

Joshua 24:15 is my decision again today. I love and honor you.

— *Day 16* —

Thank you, Lord, for your Joshua 1:5 and 9 promises. You won't leave me or forsake me and you will be with me wherever I go. You are faithful and don't make idle promises; you keep them all. Top it off with "You are the Omega" who is sovereign. Thank you.

Lord, I want you to transform me to be more like you. (2 Corinthians 3:18). Sanctify me through and through. I can't transform myself; only the Holy Spirit has the power to make the changes in my life that YOU want made. You tell me that the Holy Spirit is working in me, giving me the desire to do what pleases you. (Philippians 2:13). Nudge me with your gentle whisper (1 Kings 19:12) or whatever it takes; I want to hear you. I want to be Christ-like.

Lord, I know you live in me; you are here. You came when I asked you to be my Lord and Savior. I am asking you to live through me. (Colossians 1:27). You are my only hope of glory.

Today, may I make choices that reflect you and your love in each situation. Then, Lord, I ask you to grow my trust and help me have your power, love, faith and wisdom to become like you. I know those things are in me because you live in me. Give me a fresh awareness of your presence and your power. May your Spirit work a miracle in me to be more like you.

I want to become more sensitive to your leading as I live out my Joshua 24:15 decision. You alone control what happens. I will seek you as I go and be at peace.

You are due all my love, honor, praise, and thanksgiving.

— *Day 17* —

Lord, I cannot stop thanking you for being you or for all the blessings you have provided for me—nor do I want to. And in the same breath, I cannot stop asking for more. Lord, you made me "in your image" (Genesis 1:27); and now I am asking you to make me more and more Christ-like each day. I am created to be like you in true righteousness and holiness. (Ephesians 4:24).

I am to love you with all my heart, soul, and mind and my neighbor as myself. (Matthew 22:37-40). Lord, use your Word to guide me in each situation as I encounter your other children. Your Word gives me truth, other people give me support as I grow, and the situation gives me an opportunity to practice being Christ-like. Thank you. Lord, help me learn to give "thanks in everything."

I want to learn to love like you love. You love the world, even those who are difficult to love—including me. You loved from the cross and there couldn't have been a more difficult situation.

Thank you for your Holy Spirit within me reminding me of your Word that you have already written on my heart; I want you to write more. Thank you for your intercessory prayer when I don't know how to pray. Thank you for the opportunity to practice loving all your children in every situation.

Yes, help me learn to give thanks in everything. Yes, I thank you for growing me to be Christ-like. Right know, I am just an ugly caterpillar but someday I'll be a beautiful butterfly. Thank you.

My decision is still Joshua 24:15 and I am asking you to bind Satan from "me and mine" so we can serve you as you would want. My love, praise and honor belong to you.

— Day 18 —

Thank you again, Lord for all your faithfulness and especially for meeting me each morning. What a wonderful way for me to start the day—with you. May I continue throughout the day to breathe in your presence, to hold tightly to your hand, and to go with you. You said, "Follow me." and I want to do just that. (John 21:19).

I am telling you my own wants and wishes—sometimes I even pray for someone else's healing, sadness, loss. Today I am also asking for spiritual growth through each and every circumstance; may I be drawn closer to you. Refine me—make me more Christ-like in any problem you don't remove. (2 Corinthians 4:17). Grow me, Lord.

Lord, your church needs you every day—your love, guidance, leadership, strength, courage, unity. We need your love most of all...each and every day. And, missionaries everywhere, persecuted Christians, and other souls around the world—we all need you! Your kingdom needs their King. "Your kingdom come. Your will be done on earth as it is in heaven." (Matthew 6:10). Thank you for answering my prayers in ways that I may never see. I just know you hear and you answer when my prayers are in agreement with your divine plan.

You don't change; thank you. You are my strength just like you were Habakkuk's (3:19). You made this day; I will rejoice and be glad in it (Psalm 118:24) as I continue in my decision to serve you. (Joshua 24:15).

Forgive me for I sin against you—fail you so often—yet I do love and praise you.

— *Day 19* —

Lord, today may I receive your blessings gratefully. As I seek your face, (Psalm 27:8) your blessing of peace settles over me. Thank you. As I look around at your handiwork, I see your blessings everywhere— just as you are everywhere. You yourself are my greatest blessing! It is wonderful when the sense of your wholeness fills me. (Philippians 4:7).

When all my "wonderfully laid" plans are thwarted, I quickly come to you saying "Fix this" or even "Fix me" because I know I am inadequate and need your strength and guidance. Help me be just as quick to come to you when all my plans are working on "my" schedule. It is only by your grace they are going as "I" planned—your permissive will. Truly, I want to learn to give thanks in all things.

Never let my awareness of your presence fade into the background. You are the Light that shines in every situation and on every circumstance. You are always there, watching and waiting even as I often function as though I were alone. May my focus grow to include you in all my moments.

Lord, each day as I reaffirm my decision to serve you (Joshua 24:15), I ask you to grow an intense love in me and in each of my family for you.

May we reverently fear your holy name and love our neighbors as you directed so that my decision is played out according to your will. I also include your church in Longview and all around the world when I ask for this intense love for you. May we find strength, courage, guidance and peace as we honor you in service and unity.

This day is yours. I will rejoice in it (Psalm 118:24) as I love, honor, praise and give thanks to you.

— *Day 20* —

Thank you for going out of your way to be with me just as you went out of your way to be with the woman at the well. (John 4:7-26). Thank you now for all the good that will come later; you have plans to "prosper me." (Jeremiah 29:11). May my plans fit into yours which are higher—bigger, better—than mine. (Isaiah 55:8-9). I seek you and your will for me.

Lord, you don't hide your face from me—nor do you reject me. (Psalm 88:4). You are always with me; (Joshua 1:5,9); I so want to hold onto that truth. In times of deep frustration and pain of disappointment, Satan spouts his lies over and over that you have left me to fend for myself, that you don't care about me or hear my prayers. His lies cloud my vision of you and he attempts to drown out your voice. You and my Father are omnipotent and omnipresent, and your rose from the grave victorious; therefore, I am asking you to hold me close to you as you tenderly reassure me of your presence and love.

You are the answer to my every frustration and disappointment. Help me seek you in all the hidden places—in things I don't understand. Give me a deeper revelation of you. Give me wisdom and grace to come to you with open hands to receive and accept whatever it is you have for me. May I love you above all else.

Lord, one minute I say, "Thank you" and the next "Help me, Give me." Even in that shallowness and weakness, my decision is the same: Joshua 24:15. In your name, I am shutting Satan's mouth and binding him. I am yours! I love, honor, and praise you for holding me securely in your right hand.

— *Day 21* —

Lord, my security rests in you alone; I want to be all yours—free from any other dependency. The tenderness of your everlasting arms softens any pain and your strength holds me. (Romans 8:39).

Lord, I love your message to me in Hebrews 11 and the review of the faithful giants through the ages: Abel (4), Enoch (5), Noah (7), Abraham (8), Sarah (11), Jacob (21), Joseph (22), Moses and his parents (22-23), and others. David didn't question his faith; he just knew you would triumph. I don't question my faith—it's my obedience that's lacking.

By faith, Abraham went when he didn't know where he was going. (8). You are calling each day for me to "take up my cross and follow you. (Luke 9:23). Like Abraham, I don't know where that leads; but, Lord, I want to be like Abraham when he "obeyed and went." (8).

You are Lord of the universe as well as my Lord and Savior. Help me start today being obedient in forgiving others as you have forgiven my multiple offenses. As I seek you each morning, learn your Word, become willing to obey and go, may I recognize your guidance.

Today let me be a lifeline to someone who needs you, who needs encouragement, who needs to know you. May I see each person I encounter as you see them—someone you created in your image. We are all in need of something special; ***gospel truth and your love***. May that flow through me today to others!

Today I am asking you to lead our nation's leaders, make them fully aware of you. (1 Timothy 2:2-3). May your people humble themselves, pray, seek you, and repent so that our land may be healed. (2 Chronicles 7:14). Adding to the list: church, city, state leaders. And, family leaders as well as me. My decision is made: Joshua 24:15. You have my love, praise, and thanks.

— *Day 22* —

Lord, today as I hold your hand, help me accept things exactly as they are and give thanks. May I embrace the challenges, grow closer to you, and graciously receive all the blessings you have for me. I want to trust in your "unfailing love forever and ever." (Psalm 5:28). May I "lean on, trust in, and be confident in you with all my heart and mind—and in everything put you first." (Proverbs 3:4-6).

Lord, I do believe in your Word and I know you "will not withhold good things from your children whom you love and who are following you." (Psalm 84:11). So often I sound like a spoiled brat saying, "Lord, if you really loved me, you'll give me what I want." I seem to forget you are omniscient and that I can trust you even when you don't give me what I ask for. Why do I find it so hard to see "your withholdings" as true evidence of your love?

I don't comprehend your ways, Lord; you are all knowing and all wise as well as sovereign. Your ways are too wonderful for me to know (Job 42:3). They are higher than all else. (Isaiah 55:8-9). Help me find rest while not knowing, just accepting your ways and trusting in you who knows all.

And, I must not forget to thank you for all the good things you do not withhold from me, as well as learn to thank you for those you do withhold. Never let me listen to Satan's lies as he tries to sow seeds of doubt about your love for me as you withhold certain things.

I do trust that you love me and know what you are doing. "You give and you take away. I praise your name." (Job 1:21).

My decision today is the same as yesterday's: to serve you.

— *Day 23* —

Thank you for being here for this TAG! I can never thank you enough even as I repeat and repeat and repeat. Thank you for seeing me as I am: a wrinkled, gray haired, saggy-skinned old woman who loves you. (Psalm 92:12-15; Proverbs 31:30).

Yes, Lord, I want to stay healthy and look presentable; but most of all, I want my heart to be presentable you. I want to have a gentle, quiet spirit (1 Peter 3:4) that will glorify you—as I thank you for the time you have given me. My worth and purpose lie in the truth that I am "your image bearer"; it is there that I fail you so often. Help me learn to reflect your beauty, your person, your work as you want me to.

May I age by and in your grace. May I live this day holding onto your hand and your promises for me. May I be more concerned with reflecting your love and how I can make an impact with your "good news" than I am with erasing the laugh lines from years of joy with you.

Lord, as I continue to grow older, may I spend my years close to you and show others the beauty that lies in that horrible cross. May I be a channel of blessing that draws others to you. May I be of use to you today and every day until you come to take me home to be with you there. My decision of Joshua 24:15 is still intact.

And I am committing to follow your instructions in 1 Timothy 2:2. I am praying for our leaders and those in authority: national, state, city, church and especially family leaders...and add J and K as they start a new life as husband and wife. All my cares are in your powerful right hand. My love and praise go to you.

— *Day 24* —

Lord, never let me grow tired of thanking you for my TAG's. Being aware that I am in the presence of the Creator of the universe who loves and cares for me is wonderful beyond words. I can rejoice and be grateful that your love has no limits and no conditions. And, thank you for allowing me to whisper your name throughout the day and find this same peace I have now. Calling out to you, calms the fears that surface when I see all the chaos all around me. (Deuteronomy 31:6).

Lord, I love the song that says "without a problem, I would never know what you can do." I give you so many opportunities to show your strength and power because I have so many weaknesses. (2 Corinthians 12:9). I want my faith and trust to grow so others can see you at work. In all honesty, I want to see your miracles! I want to live each day expecting a miracle! I know you are performing them! I want to live so close to you—so in tune with you—that I recognize them. Open my eyes, Lord.

Oh, how our nation and our leaders need you—just as I do. May we all look to you for guidance, strength, and courage.

Again, Joshua 24:15...with my love, praise, and thanks going to you.

— *Day 25* —

Lord, thank you for life itself, but also for life in you. I am nothing without you. You went out of your way to go to Samaria to meet the woman at the well. (John 4: 5+). Thank you for going to Calvary for me and thank you more for your victory over death and the grave.

Lord, my prayer this morning is Mark 4:19: "Never let the attraction of this world, the delights of wealth, the search for success and the lure of nice things come in and crowd out your Word to me." Never let anything come before my love for you. Hold me close.

And, Lord, when I don't know what "step to take/decision to make," remind me to bring everything to you in prayer. You tell me "Keep asking...and Keep searching..."so I can be certain you did not mean for me to ask once and forget about it. Lord, I need your help. I want to learn how to apply your Word—not misapply—to every detail of my life—every circumstance—every encounter.

Lord, thank you for all your blessings! Help me be full of joy in the "labors of life," giving thanks for it all. You have been so merciful to me; I don't deserve such mercies. I want to know the full meaning of "joy in you to be my strength" in the tough times of life—so others will have hope and you will be glorified.

Again, Joshua 24:15 is my decision. And, again I ask for your power to bind Satan from me and my house—also from our nation's leaders.

Love, honor, and praise go to you.

— *Day 26* —

Lord, you are here with me this morning. You know that I am feeling the loss of my closest friend and you care. Thank you. You felt Mary's and Martha's pain when their brother died and you wept. (John 11:35). You understood; he was your friend. You understand now.

Somehow I slip into a fantasy expectation that I deserve and will have a problem-free life or that "I" can resolve all the difficulties. You remind me that in this world there will be trouble. (John 16:33). I thank you that Neta now has a problem-free, pain-free life with you forever. She believed in you as the Son of God. Thank you for the years of friendship we shared; it was a special gift.

This day I want to enjoy your presence and glorify you. I don't understand omnipresence, but I believe Neta is with you and you are also with me. May I always remain steadfast, trusting you. (Psalm 112:4). Fill me this day with love, joy, peace, patience, kindness, goodness, faithfulness, gentleness, and self-control—the fruit of the Spirit—You. (Galatians 5:22-23). Fill me to overflowing so others know it comes from you and be encouraged.

I ask for guidance. May I recognize "the someone you want me to touch today—someone who needs encouragement, needs to be lifted up. I am yours; use me.

Lord, I ask that you give our nation and its leaders special guidance, strength, courage to stand with you, know you. We need you desperately. Unify our nation—and let the unity be in you. Now, even closer: may our city, church, and family be unified in you.

My decision today is Joshua 24:15. Lord, in the power of your name, not mine, I am binding Satan from me and my family. All love, honor, praise, and thanksgiving are to you.

— *Day 27* —

Lord, did you wake me early (3:20 a.m.) so I would be available for our TAG? If so, I thank you. If not, I'm still glad I'm here with you. I need you to soften my heart and settle my soul before I begin class today. May my interaction with each one of your children that I meet be a reflection of you. Let today be to your glory, not mine!

Thank you for who you are: Son of God. Fully God and yet fully human. ???—No, I don't understand it, but I accept it. Thank you for being the "God of Fresh Starts." (2 Corinthians 5:17). Thank you that I can have access to the Heavenly Father at any moment because of you. Through you, I don't have to wait for the high priest to make a sacrifice for me. You paid it all—and my "thank you" isn't nearly enough. My sin is "as far away from me as the east is from the west." (Psalm 103:12). What a fresh start!

This morning I am asking you to do the same thing for me that David asked you to do for him: "Create a new, clean heart in me—filled with right desires." (Psalm 51:10). And then "Restore to me the joy of your salvation and give me a willing/sustaining spirit." (51:12). You did that for David and I am trusting you to do that for me also.

Lord, yes, everything new: my mind—to think your thoughts; my body— to live for you; my mouth—to speak healing words of encouragement; my hands—to serve others; my heart—to seek you above all else.

My decision is Joshua 24:15 so I am asking you to bind Satan from me and my house. Draw our nation and its leaders to you. May we repent of our evil ways and turn to you.

You are due all my love, honor, praise, and thanksgiving.

— *Day 28* —

Lord, you are the living, loving God who never changes. You are with me always. (Matthew 28:20). You send protective angels for me just as you did for Daniel in the lions' den. (Daniel 6:16-21). You send devout believers to mentor me just as you sent Mordicai to guide Esther. Lord, I am so grateful you never change and are forever faithful.

Your teachings are true and perfect, and I want to learn to apply them in my daily life. Without faith, I cannot please you; (Hebrews 11:6); but it is you who rewards my faith. Give me wisdom to live in humble submission to you, each day, where I live, recognizing your guidance. Lord, I want to be obedient and faithful to you.

It is only when you are my focus that my days have meaning. I want to see the world from your perspective and be obedient to you. When everything is going "my way," it is easy to be obedient. But when there is a "major bump in the road" and my dream vanishes, I need your support, encouragement, guidance to be obedient. I always need you.

I think of Joseph's engagement and his expectations for his honeymoon. In an instant, his whole world was turned upside down; there isn't supposed to be a pregnant fiancé. But, Joseph chose to be obedient, to do what God told him to do. He took Mary to be his wife—even though he did not understand.

Lord, I want to be obedient: to love, to trust, to take action under your guidance. Even as old as I am, I want to serve you: Joshua 24:15. In your name, I am binding Satan from me and my family for your glory. I love you, Lord.

— *Day 29* —

Lord, thank you for speaking to me over and over again when I don't hear you the first time. Thank you for using different means of getting my attention. (Job 33:14-16). You use people, sermons, nature, but it is your Word that guides me most often.

Teach me to meditate on your Word: teach me the art of digging out—hearing/seeing—what you have for me. Colossians 4:2 tells me to devote myself to prayer: stay alert, watch for answers, and give thanks. Lord, I want to see your messages to me that are quietly resting as golden nuggets of scripture.

I want to devote myself to prayer: talk to you about everything before, after, and during "the situation." You are always there: omnipresent. You already know more about "the situation" than I do—every detail and what lies ahead: omniscient. You are sovereign—in total control: omnipotent. Most of all, you love me. You died for me.

Help me stay alert, watching for your answers. You know how quickly I let the world distract me. You want me to see you first and stay focused. You want me to see you at work on my behalf. Lord, you want me to have an attitude of thanksgiving. Now, Lord, let my wants be the same as yours. Let your Word guide me through this day and my actions be pleasing to you. And help me give thanks to you in every situation.

This day is yours; I will rejoice in it. I will look for you in every person I meet. And Joshua 24:15 is my prayer. I love you, honor you, praise you, and give you thanks.

— *Day 30* —

Lord, thank you for..., thank you for..., yes, the list goes on and on. Every gift I have came from you. The greatest gift I have is your loving presence. Then there is your Word that never changes. Thank you for all your reassurances that give me strength.

I just discovered Isaiah 46:4: "You promise to be with me for a lifetime, even though my hair turns white. You made me and will care for me. You will carry me along and be my Savior." How can I have a worry? Your Word is fresh and new each morning—much like the manna you provided your people in the desert. It gives me strength, but I must come to you each day to be fed.

Your were committed to listening and talking to our Father, your Father. I want to be like you, but I want it for myself. I want to acknowledge the Father for who he is. I come to you, since you and the Father are one, asking for basic needs: forgiveness of my sins and protection from Satan in all his disguises. Instill in me a desire to hear and obey your commands, to ask and receive your favor, and to go tell the "good news."

Everything around me is changing so rapidly once again; you know that! Thank you for never changing—always being the same—and for always being with me—and for caring about the losses I am feeling. You wept for Mary and Martha. Once again, you don't change; you weep for me too!

You know my decision is Joshua 24:15. Love, honor, praise belong to you.

— *Day 31* —

Lord, I love you. I thank you for being you and all that you are. Thank you for all the gifts and blessings you have given me and continue to give me. Thank you for your presence this a.m. and for your Word. It is only in you that I can "Always be joyful." (1 Thessalonians 5:16). Today, I just "Keep on praying." (5:17). And, I ask you to teach me to be "Thankful no matter what happens." (5:18).

Lord, I want each of my family and others to know my heart and see me trusting you each day. I have complete, immediate access to your Throne of Grace, so let them see me rejoice in you. Let them know I acknowledge you as sovereign and go to you for strength and comfort in every situation. Let them see me giving thanks—being thankful because you provide undeserved blessings over and over—*for your glory, not mine.*

Lord, I want to know how to pray for my family, my church, Buckner, this nation. Teach me. May I have a "spiritual transaction" with you each day. I give you my anger, frustration, anxiety in exchange for your peace. Thank you.

As for now, I reaffirm my Joshua 24:15 decision and ask that you bind Satan in whatever disguise the deceiver chooses to use today. I am yours.

Love, honor, praise, and thanks all belong to you.

Again I Come to You

— *Day 1* —

Lord, I know I can come fearlessly to the Throne of Grace and into God's presence expecting a glad welcome because I come with you in trust. (Ephesians 3:12). Let my focus be on you and you alone, fully aware of who you are and all that you have done.

You are the God of creation who is awesome and holy. Let there be a dialogue between us as I listen for your voice. I earnestly seek you and pray Psalm 63:1. I so want a constant awareness of your presence in my life; I need your loving touch.

In all this, let me thank you for your presence with me now—today— this minute. As I look ahead, I become fearful; forgive me. If there is an abyss in my path, you are there and what else do I need? "You will provide your angels to accompany, defend and preserve me in my obedient walk with you." (Psalm 91:11-12). And, if it is a mountain to climb instead of an abyss, you and your angels will be there, too.

I am not alone now and I won't be alone in the future. I want to learn to "walk by faith and not by sight" (2 Corinthians 57); and you, Lord, know that is foreign to my nature.

David tells me that "with your help, he can advance against a troop, and with you, he can scale a wall." (Psalm 18:29). Lord, with faith like that, it is no wonder he was a man after your heart. I want faith like that.

I am a weakling, but my decision is still to serve you. (Joshua 24:15). Thank you for binding Satan and giving me strength and courage to serve you.

Lord, how could I not love you!

— *Day 2* —

Lord, you tell me I can come to you when I feel weary and burdened and find rest with you. (Matthew 11:28). Thank you. If I am aware of your presence with me, I am renewed/refreshed. It is only when I focus on obligations and unsolved problems and lose sight of you that I feel overwhelmed.

I only have two requirements: to love you and others as myself, (Matthew 22:37-40) and that is not a burden. It is a privilege. When loving you becomes my highest priority, other things on my agenda lose their importance, their power and control over me.

Lord, if I am anxious, I have let something or someone become more important to me than you—something has come between us. Forgive me. I want to love you with all my heart, soul, and mind—desperately. I don't want to waste my time and energy on lesser pursuits.

You tell me to bring all things to you in prayer. If I am the one you want to use "to do something" or "to be responsible for something," you will infuse me with the power, strength, and guidance to get it done as I stay close to you in prayer. And I will know that it is you calling me. Again in your power, it will not be a burden.

You won't ask me to do anything without providing your power and direction to get it done, but I have to come to you for that!

Today, may I "Look to you and your strength." As David says, I am to "Seek your face always." (Psalm 105:4). Lord, transform me by renewing my mind in you each day. (Romans 12:1-2). I do love you even though I fail you often.

Joshua 24:15 is still my decision and I need you to bind Satan from me and my house—please.

— *Day 3* —

Lord, thank you again this morning for a TAG! I believe you may have brought me to this place for me to be more focused on you. May everything in my life revolve around you, my living Lord. You are the center of time—BC-AD, the center of history, the center of life—meaning, purpose. Nothing really matters except you and your will.

My relationship with you must be my focus—does that mean I am taking away from you at the center? Am I still too consumed with me and mine? I do thank you for all your blessings—all you have done for me, but then I immediately ask you to do something else as though you exist for my personal benefit. Forgive me, Lord.

I want to want you more. I want to want what you want. May what you think matter more to me than what anyone else thinks—and that includes what I think. I want to be available for your use. I want to be a part of your plan—and not just ask you to come be a part of my plan.

I am yours. Lord, Father in heaven, I believe you hear me because I come to you in the name of your Son, Jesus—who created all things, who is the exact representation of you, who shed his blood for me. I come to you because you invited me, because his blood opened the door for me to come in, and because his blood washed me and cleansed me. You will listen to me because I belong to your Son. He is my reason for living. Yes, Father, I come to you in the name of Jesus.

My love, praise, honor and thanksgiving are due you.

— *Day 4* —

Lord, today, I am in "bits and pieces"—no continuity, just a thought here and there. First, I love you deeply and want to be closer to you. Thank you for this TAG; yes, I repeat.

I fail you and I ask forgiveness. Your Word, your love, prayers of others —present and years past—have brought me to this place. Sometimes I think your loving discipline is severe, harsh, and unfeeling when things don't change. I seem to think "Lord, I am being good, why do you do this to me?" Just how "spoiled brat" can I be!

You aren't trying to make me comfortable; you want to build my character. Somehow I haven't fully grasped how much it cost you to go to the cross for me or how horrible it was for our Father to watch you die on my behalf—for the likes of me! Ugh. And, somehow I don't grasp how horrible my sin really is! Forgive me.

You are perfection and your blood cleansed me once and for all time. Grow me now in faith and trust so that I fully surrender, submit, accept your way as perfect! Teach me. Hold me close to you as I learn.

I am in this new family—adopted into your Kingdom as your child. I am a sister to you, Lord, and a daughter of my heavenly Father. And this new family—*I've only been in this family about 70 years*— has new ways, and I want to understand all the new ways you have for me. I am never alone; I am fully loved and cared for. Help me grow to be like you—recognizable in this world as yours.

Transform me so that **You** are able to reveal **Yourself** to others through me. Use me. I am dependent on you, the Father and your Spirit. And, my decision is Joshua 24:15. My love, honor, praise and thanksgiving go to you.

— *Day 5* —

Lord, I am yours and you are mine forever—my Lord and Savior. You give me this time with you and I thank you for it. I want more of it—not less. I want to learn to take this awareness I have of you with me into encounters I have with others of "our" family.

You are the Lord of creation; you hung the stars in space and you are here with me. ***Wow!*** Thank you. You created light and you shine forever without change or shadow. (James 1:17). You are faithful to generation after generation; may I become more faithful to you and share your love with those around me now for the next generation.

Your timing is perfect, even though I seldom know it at the moment. Even when I see no evidence that you are intervening on my behalf, I want to trust you. You hear and answer my prayers. (Jeremiah 29:12-13). Just because I can't visibly see the answer yet, I trust you are answering because I believe your Word.

Lord, help me trust you fully, completely, whole heartedly, graciously when the answer is not what I wanted to hear—not ***the way*** I wanted my prayer answered—not ***when*** I wanted it answered. I am trusting that your greatness has not been diluted since the beginning of time; you are the same yesterday, today, and forever—answering prayers on GPT.

Now I ask you to strip me of my pride, Lord. Shine your light into my heart and let me see myself evaluated against your standard. Remove any self-righteousness and all my judgmental attitudes. Teach me to pray so Heaven is moved and my heart becomes like yours.

I love, praise, honor, and give thanks to you. My decision is still Joshua 24:15 and in your name I pray.

— *Day 6* —

Lord, this morning instead of thanking you for this TAG, I am thanking you for this manna! That is what this time with you is to me: it's your daily provision for me. It feeds me and gives me strength, but I must come each day to receive its benefits. I just know I thank you for it.

Thank you for creating me "in your image" (Genesis 1:26), but my sin(s) damaged any resemblance there was of you. Thank you for re-creating me through your death and resurrection. The moment when I came to you—the Son of God—asking forgiveness of my sin, you started the process of recreating me. This re-creation is a much slower process than the creation. Thank you for not giving up on me.

Thank you for this day-by-day process of renewing me inwardly through this manna you provide: your presence, your Word, time together, prayer, other Christians. Though I grow impatient because I continue to mess up your "handiwork", I want to remember I can come to you for more grace. You continue to make all things new! And you always finish what you start. Thank you.

Then, one day I will see you Face to face. Until then, I will come to you in faith to feed on your Word—to grow closer to you—the God of creation. When you are finished with me—your re-creation—and I see you in person, I will be a beautiful reflection of your glory—perfect and complete. I don't understand it all and you know that, Lord; but *I believe it*. At that time, I will be forever praising you! Today I will love, honor, praise, and give thanks in my limited ability. Forgive me when I fail you.

My decision is still Joshua 24:15. In your omnipotence, I ask you to bind Satan from me and each of my house so others may see your reflection in us.

— *Day 7* —

Psalm 23

Lord, you are my Shepherd—
> That's ***Relationship!***

You make me lie down in green pastures—
> That's ***Rest!***

You lead me beside still waters—
> That's ***Refreshment!***

You restore my soul!
> That's ***Healing!***

You lead me in the paths of righteousness—
> That's ***Guidance!***

For your name's sake—
> That's ***Purpose!***

Even though I walk through the valley of the shadow of death—
> That's ***Testing!***

I will fear no evil—
> That's ***Protection!***

For You are with me—
> That's ***Faithfulness!***

Your rod and your staff, they comfort me—
> That's ***Discipline!***

You prepare a table before me in the presence of my enemies—
> That's ***Hope!***

You anoint my head with oil—
> That's ***Consecration!***

My cup overflows—
> That's ***Abundance!***

Surely love and mercy shall follow me all the days of my life—
> That's ***Blessing!***

And I will dwell in the house of the Lord—
> That's ***Security!***

Forever—
> That's ***Eternity!***

Lord, may I thank you with service.

— *Day 8* —

Thank you, Lord, for being here with me this morning. I know you are here; but, Lord, I am struggling to sense your presence. My thoughts are scattered. I just know I love you, I fail you, I need you!

I am seeking your face as I start this day; I want your peace—the peace that only you can provide. I am asking your Spirit that is in me to control my mind (Romans 8:6) as I hold tightly to your hand and let you guide me.

Your Word never gets old: "You are my refuge and strength, ever-present help." (Psalm 46:1-2). Thank you. I am lifting up my hands in faith (1 Timothy 2:8) for your Presence to fill my emptiness. Lord, I want your Light, as well as, your Joy, Peace, Love, Kindness, Gentleness, all of your fruit to flow to me, fill me, and flow through me. (Galatians 6:22-23).

Today must be a day to surrender/submit once again. I am bone-weary, spent, at the end of me! I cannot effect change anywhere on my own. Help me—my go-to prayer—accept the situation as it is at this moment and completely trust you and your sovereignty. You can fit—and are fitting—all things into your plan for good. (Romans 8:28).

What would I do, Lord, without the assurances of your promises! Not a question—just a statement of awe! I know I would fail completely, forever. "Mary—your mama, Lord—treasured God's Word in her heart. (Luke 2:19). I treasure your promises also.

Joshua 24:15 is my decision this morning. In your name I am binding Satan from me and mine at this moment so we can be of use to you. All my love, honor, praise go to you.

— Day 9 —

Lord, I come this morning "thanking and asking" just as is my usual pattern. I sincerely thank you for who you are and for all you have done for me. But, then I immediately begin to ask for something! It sounds so phony—even to me. It's not. It's real! I know that all good gifts come from you. I am nothing without you and I don't deserve the blessings you have provided; i.e. being able to be with my children. Thank you, but thank you isn't enough.

Lord, when something seems so hopeless and wasted, I don't know where to go with that except to you—surrendering the whole situation to you. You in your infinite grace and divine sovereignty know all things from beginning to end. You know my every thought and my every step. You, who raised people from the dead and even rose from the grave yourself, can pick up broken pieces and fix "it"—whatever it is!

You waste nothing. Whatever I believe about wasted time and wasted, useless lives doesn't matter. It is what I believe about you that matters. You work all things together for the good of those who love you and are called according to your purpose." (Romans 8:28).

I want to know all your promises and "rest on" them. I am able to rest on them because you are the Alpha and the Omega, Beginning and End, First and Last, my Savior, my sovereign Shepherd, my Counselor, my Comforter, my Deliverer, my Foundation, my Fortress, my Redeemer, my sustaining Provider. I am yours and you love me.

Today I need you to "fix me" so I am not useless. I want to keep my commitment to serve you. (Joshua 24:15). In your name I am binding Satan from me and my house so you can use me.

All praise and honor belong to you.

— Day 10 —

Lord, this morning I come praising you, honoring you, loving you, thanking you; but then it seems my thoughts are scattered and words will not come. I read a portion of your Word and I want to talk to you about that message. I read another portion and I want to talk to you about that thought. Maybe I just need to listen for your voice. (John 10:27).

Aries, my precious—60-pound, pit bull—lap dog knows my voice. It does not matter how many voices are involved or how much noise is going on, he can pick out my voice. Before I open the door—before he sees me, he is delighted and ready to greet me whole heartedly. He can pick out my voice because we spend a lot of time together and he belongs to me. I am his mistress!

Lord, I wonder if I am half as good at hearing and recognizing your voice, my Master's voice? As I abide in you, help me hear your voice above all the other voices and the endless distractions. I believe you still speak primarily through scripture, but also through others of your children, nature, circumstances. I want to hear you and know your voice.

Thank you for reassuring me that I will find you when I earnestly seek you and you are listening to me. (Jeremiah 29:12-13). Lord, I want you to lead me daily. (2 Timothy 3:16-17).

Lord, I want to be like Aries is at this moment: He is lying patiently content at my feet waiting for me—his mistress—to move or not move—to call his name or be silent. But, he will react joyously and be ready to go when I am ready.

Thank you, Lord, for getting your point across to me through Aries. Use whatever tool you choose, but draw me close to you.

I love, honor, and praise you.

— Day 11 —

Lord, thank you for being here with me now; you are everything I need. (Psalm 23:1). Lord, I want a deep, powerful love relationship with you—and, Lord, let it be so strong others will see you in it and through it. May your strength show through me to give you honor. (Psalm 23:2-3).

Thank you for walking with me in troubled times, for guarding and guiding me. (4-5). Help me follow you closely or hold tightly to your hand as you lead me. Many of my greatest blessings come in times of pain and turmoil—those blessings are your presence and your teachings. Thank you.

Again, I thank you for never leaving me even when I strayed from you. Your goodness and unfailing kindness have been constant and will be to the end. (6) You are the Omega! Thank you for paying the price for my salvation and for the promise you gave the thief on the cross: "He would be with you in paradise." That promise gives a wonderful assurance to me.

Lord, I have often been too quick with words. You entrusted me with this power. (Proverbs 18:21). May I be so filled with your fruit (Galatians 5:22-23) that every word I speak is filtered through your Word and has the power to lift and encourage. May I speak peace, joy, self-control so you are honored and others are blessed.

I just want to keep my Joshua 24:15 commitment. In your name I am binding Satan from this house.

My love, honor, praise, and thanks go to you.

— *Day 12* —

Thank you, Lord, for this day. Your blessings are too numerous to count—like grains of sand on the beach! Yet, it is your presence that is my greatest blessing.

Forgive me when I fail you. Lord, keep me from being a "Functional Atheist." Keep me from functioning as though I am alone and as though "it all" depends on me. You are always with me. Keep me from viewing a situation without recognizing you are in it with me. Keep me from acting to resolve a situation before I ask you for your guidance. Keep me from acting as though your laws don't apply to me and as if there will be no consequences for my disobedience. Yes, forgive my sins as I am humbly sorry and want to please you. Help me see every encounter as an opportunity to share your love and give encouragement.

Any problem is a learning opportunity that is only limited by my willingness to be teachable. Help me keep my eyes and heart open to all that you are doing and give you "thanks in all things." Help me see any and all "trials, troubles, difficulties" as preparation for your glory. You went to the cross and to hell; those were horrible happenings, but today I can give thanks for them because you rose victoriously from the grave. Help me learn "to give thanks in all things." (2 Corinthians 4:17 and 1 Thessalonians 5:18).

I am weak and need you to strengthen me. I praise you, love you, and want to honor you as I give my cares to you.

— *Day 13* —

Lord, thank you, thank you, thank you! The list of your gifts and blessings is too long to put here, but I thank you. Let me start this day acknowledging you made this day and I will rejoice in it. (Psalm 118:24).

You know I am a lifelong worrier; but, Lord, I repent and am trying to learn to be fully in the present—in the now with you—to keep my eyes focused on you. I don't want to miss the blessings you have placed around me because I am looking ahead and leaving you out of the picture.

You have provided abundantly more than I could have thought to ask for or even imagine. (Ephesians 3:20). Thank you. Help me see you everywhere and in everything I experience today. (Matthew 6:33). You direct my steps and give me what I need.

Yes, I have experienced loss, grief, pain, and heartache; but you comfort me. (2 Corinthians 1:4). May I learn to comfort others. I want to know you more intimately, deeply than ever before. Though it hurts to see my children in pain, it is through pain that God, the Father, does his greatest work and reveals himself to me and to them. Thank you. Lord, as I surrender to you in this journey, I ask you to do your work in and through me. Lord, thank you for speaking to me over and over again and in different ways. (Job 33:14-18). I want to hear your voice over and above anyone else's. I want you to guide me. May I practice constant expectant prayers giving thanks (Colossians 4:2) as I stay committed to my Joshua 24:15 decision.

All love, honor, praise and thanksgiving go to you. Lord, I beg you to use your power to bind Satan from me and my house.

— *Day 14* —

Lord, I can never thank you enough for all that you did so I could know the Father and have peace. May I wear your peace with dignity and allow it to keep me—my heart and mind—close to you (John 20:19-21 and 14:27) so I can walk boldly throughout the day—everyday. And may you continue to be with me, allowing me to find strength and courage in your presence.

Lord, you and I know Satan is not running around in a red suit; he is a liar and a master of disguises. He is fear and worry. When I ask you to bind him—I am asking you to bind him in every form (anger, greed, envy, jealousy, etc.) from me and my family. I am committed to serving you. (Joshua 24:15).

Thank you for giving me every reason to be confident in you and your presence with me. You have never failed me. I just want to keep my eyes fixed on you as you are sitting victoriously at our Father's throne. (Hebrews 12:2). Yes, being with the Father and at the same time being here with me is beyond my understanding; but I accept the fact that you are omnipresent! Thank you. Yes, you take hold of my hand and tell me not to fear because you will help me. (Isaiah 41:13). Thank you that you never change!

May I give myself wholeheartedly to this day—being a glory to you, honoring you, loving you and others, encouraging each person I meet. Use me. Guide me. I don't want to run ahead of you and get in your way.

I am yours. I love you.

— *Day 15* —

Thank you, Lord, for this special time with you, this TAG! I am with the God of creation, the Risen Lord, the Alpha and the Omega, the Great I Am, the omnipotent, omniscient, omnipresent loving Father and his Son. Lord, I am weak and can't seem to hold onto you; I simply rest in the peace that you are holding onto me.

Nothing is impossible with you. (Luke 1:37). I don't know what the specific answer is to some of life's situations, but I know you do and I rest in that. (Ephesians 3:20). You are my Shepherd and you love, guide, and restore me just as you did David. (Psalm 23:1-4).

Lord, my weaknesses give you the opportunity to show me your strength. Others may not view them as opportunities for miracles, but I know that without you I would surely fall (fail). You alone understand my frustration and heartache, and you alone can bring comfort in the darkest times. *A miracle*. I live in a broken world; why am I surprised when something terrible happens! And why do I think none of this will touch me! You tell me there will always be trouble on this earth and at the same time you will never leave me. *That's another miracle*.

I will rejoice in you and I will praise you with each breath I take. I will thank you because there is always an undeserved blessing in my life— starting with the salvation you bought for me with your blood.

If it is your will, use me to touch my family so that our relationships are healed. If I am not the one you choose to draw us back together and to you, close my mouth. Keep me from being a hindrance. You alone are the answer to our family's troubles, your churches' coldness, our city's issues, our state's and nation's strife—the answer to all of life!

My decision remains: Joshua 24:15! You are victorious!

— Day 16 —

Lord, as always, thank you for this TAG! May it increase my awareness of you throughout the day and enhance my faith and trust in you. I bring my repentance and lay it at your feet asking you to increase my gratitude and joy for your glory—not mine!

I want to be joyful always. May my prayers of thanksgiving be constant. (1 Thessalonians 5:16-18). Let me never lose sight of God the Father's grace and let me continue to adore you with praise and worship. Give me "holy restraint" so I don't go back and pick up the cares and concerns that I have already given you.

Lord, transform me by renewing my mind (Romans 12:2) and let me be so close to you that I have your mind. (1 Corinthians 2:15-16). Let me discuss **everything** with you. Let me exercise my faith so that it grows stronger each day. Open my eyes to see the miracles you are working this morning—because I know you are in total control. And, I repeat "You are working everything out for my good because I love you and want to fit into your plan." (Romans 8:28).

Thank you for my greatest blessing: the assurance that absolutely nothing can separate me from your love. (Romans 8:38-39).

Nothing is impossible with you (Luke 1:37) so I ask you to guide our nation and its leaders. May we repent of our sins against you and then turn to you. May our courts base its decisions on your laws. May your church remember and obey your two basic commandments—to love you and others.

May my family make a definite Joshua 24:15 decision. Lord, in your name and power, I am binding Satan from me and mine. I love, honor, and praise you with thanksgiving.

— *Day 17* —

Lord, thank you for your loving, tender mercy and grace. Forgive me for often being like "one who runs aimlessly or one beating the air." (1 Corinthians 9:26). Today I ask you, Lord, to infuse me with your power and strength to do as **you** ask. I want to be ready to do what **you** want me to do. I want to be willing to go where **you** want me to go. Let my hands be willing to **serve** others. I need **your** direction—more than that, I need **you**, Lord.

I am back to square one asking you to give me a fresh start with my focus on you. May I keep my mouth closed until you give me the words to speak. At that point, take away my anxiety and compel me to tell the Good News of your love for each of us. (John 3:16).

Lord, your grace is sufficient for all things at all times. Your strength and power have a perfect stage on which to perform in me because I am weak. (2 Corinthians 12:9). May your power and strength rest on me. Use me.

May our relationship be vibrant and challenging. I am asking you to invade every area of my life. Make me a new creation. (2 Corinthians 5:17). Transform me as I come to you each day renewing my mind in you. (Romans 12:2). May I be open to your work within me and let you alone be my security.

I am yours; use me. Remind me "the spatula stays in the drawer, clean and ready for use" until the chef reaches for it. May I be your spatula.

I love you and my decision remains: Joshua 24:15. Lord, I plead with you to bind Satan today from my family that we may be a glory to you.

— *Day 18* —

Lord, you are here with me. It is those five words that keep me and protect me from falling into despair. There have been many different spiritual altitudes in my life—from mountain tops with you to low, dry valleys wondering where are you. You didn't change. You were there with me all the time. (Joshua 1: 5, 9). In all the ebbs and flows, mountain tops and valleys, and how I may feel at any given time— the truth is God, the Father, is faithful, so are you God, the Son. You promised never to leave or forsake me—and you haven't.

May I always return to your Word and seek your counsel, omniscient Lord. Help me remember all your works as David did in Psalm 42:6— and then remember how you have acted on my own behalf through the years. When I recall your faithfulness and goodness, I have to praise and thank you. My gratitude belongs to you. I put my hope in you, my praises belong to you. You are my Savior and my God. (Psalm 42:5).

When I remember you are with me and holding me by the hand, the circumstances around me fade away. You will be with me all the way to heaven. Today, the only things I ask are for a greater awareness of you and a more intimate relationship with you as I go. (Psalm 73: 23-26).

In your name and your power, I am binding Satan from me and each of my family. You died so I could have direct access to the throne of grace. I am asking our omnipotent Father and you—the risen, victorious Savior—to bind Satan in all his disguises.

My decision to serve you (Joshua 24:15) remains and I need your power and strength of fulfill that promise.

Thanks, love, praise go to you!

— *Day 19* —

Lord, I thank you for all that you are and all that you are to me: my Savior, Lord, King, Shepherd, Foundation, Counselor, Companion, Provider, Protector, Redeemer, and on and on. You are a merciful loving God. I have sinned against you—but you already know that.

This morning, I am asking you as David did to wash me in your crimson blood and make me white as snow. (Psalm 51: 1-13). Create a new, contrite heart in me filled with right desires. (10). Restore to me the joy of your salvation, and give me a willing spirit to sustain me. (12). When my heart is right with you, my hands and feet will be ready for your use.

Today, there are those close to me who are feeling weighed down with adverse circumstances. I am asking you to guide and sustain them; reassure them of the strength and power they have in and through you. May my prayers encircle each of them that they be drawn close to you in unity. I thank you for hearing me this morning.

If my hopes and solutions for this situation are not aligned with you, if nothing turns out the way I want it to, I will still rejoice in you and praise you. (Habakkuk 3:17-19).

Lord, I don't ask you each day—as I should—to guide our nation and its leaders. May they fall on their knees repenting and asking for forgiveness. May your church also be unified in you, keeping you at its center. And, may I and my family also fall on our knees in repentance, praise, and worship.

Lord, I am reaffirming my Joshua 24:15 decision, asking you to bind Satan from me and my house. How desperately all of us—family, church, city, state, and nation—need you.

My love, praise, and thanks go to you.

— Day 20 —

Lord, I come to this time with you asking you to remind me if there is someone I have not forgiven so I can be obedient to you. You hung on the cross in the most excruciating pain and forgave us who were persecuting you. And, your Word tells me to forgive others as you forgave me. (Colossians 4:32). Lord, I want to be a reflection of you.

Today, may I be aware of your presence with me and not be afraid. (Isaiah 41:10). You hold my heart as well as my hand; may I stay true to that! Your Spirit lives in the center of me and there is your peace— not fear.

Everything and everyone around me changes, but not you. You are immutable! Today, let your Peace rule in my heart. (Colossians 3:15). You are my hope of heaven. Lord, yes, you are my hope of heaven!

You are the God of creation—awesome and holy. How can I thank you enough for all that you have done for me? How can I come expecting to have your loving arms around me and compassionately guiding me when I fail you so often? Forgive me.

I am asking you to grow my faith in all that you are and all that you are to me. I know you are with me; help me be silent and listen for your voice. Open my eyes so I see you all around me.

I am ordinary and weak, but you are awesome and holy. I want to be so close to you that I can use your strength, power, and weapons to knock down the devil's strongholds. I want to be of use to you. Use me to bring back the rebels to you. (2 Corinthians 10:3-6 and Joshua 24:15).

I am yours, Lord!

Another thought on Day 20.

Lord, you said : "I should not live on bread alone, but by every word that comes from the mouth of God." I want to learn to apply your Word to my life and let it change me to be more like you. I want to learn to share your love with others; you said "Go tell." (Matthew 28:19-20). I want to be filled to overflowing with your fruit so it can be seen and felt every time I encounter one of your children who needs a special touch. (Galatians 5:22-23).

I want a more effective study of your Word. You will teach me if I just take steps to be more diligent. Strength, courage, determination can be found in your Word.

Referencing Habakkuk 1

Lord, I do trust you even though I don't understand your patience with the evil all around me—but then your patience with me is also beyond my comprehension. I want to learn GPT. Will our nation have to become enslaved before we turn back to you? Will you use a people more evil than we are to punish our sin?

You are sovereign. May our nation see its evilness and fall to its knees asking forgiveness. May we become a Christian nation desiring to glorify you.

— *Day 21* —

Lord, I start this day seeking you first (Matthew 6:33) before my mind begins to wander—before I begin to focus on other things. I thank you for being here with me and for all your blessings. May my hands be open to receive whatever you decide to give me, knowing it is given in love.

You are an all-wise, all-knowing, loving God. And your ways are far above and beyond anything I can imagine (Isaiah 55:8-9) so help me trust you fully, give you thanks and praise, and leave the rest to you. You are able and in control!

Lord, you always provide undeserved blessings; never let me complain or criticize. May I develop in my brain deeper and deeper thought patterns of trust so you are always central in my thinking. May I be "strengthened in faith and overflowing with thankfulness." (Colossians 2:6-7). How can I not be thankful when I can "Cast all my anxiety on you simply because you love me?" (1 Peter 5:7). What Peace!

My decision remains the same: Joshua 24:15. I love you and honor you as I ask you to bind Satan from each of my family so we may glorify and serve you.

Referencing Habakkuk 2

May I be like Habakkuk and be in the best position to receive your message—in the watch tower or here on my knees. You are patient and your judgment is slow—but it is certain. (GPT). Today seems like H's time: Evil and injustice seem to have the upper hand. You hate sin more than I do; you tell me to wait patiently, trusting you. Help me live in faithfulness to you. You are still directing all things according to your purposes.

Let me never take advantage of someone's misfortune. Grow my trust in you—not in what I can do. I want nothing to be more important than you and nothing to become my idol. Only you, the one true living God, can speak—most often through your Word, but also however you choose.

May I approach you in your holy Temple—here and now, in this place with you—silently waiting to hear what you have to say to me. You are the same today as you were with Habakkuk. Thank you for never changing.

— *Day 22* —

Lord, thank you for giving me this TAG to express my thoughts and concerns. I know you care about everything that touches my life. You are a loving, compassionate listener today; back then you gave your life's blood on the cross so I could come directly to you and the Father.

May this TAG help me develop a deeper, special connection to you, the Father, and the Holy Spirit—the Trinity. May this connection give me access to the Father's direction and guidance as well as a channel for his strength to flow to me, allowing me to stand against evil. When I am linked to you and the Father through prayer, your presence and power is with me in every situation.

I want always to ask you for your wisdom, to remember your faithfulness and to see it now. When I open your Word, I discover your goodness over and over. Let me be ready to share your love with someone who needs your touch today. May I be constantly aware of your wonders, that I might boast of all that you are and all that you are doing.

Lord, my greatest strength is knowing I need you every moment! Without you I am nothing. In you, connected to you through prayer—I am joyful. (1 Thessalonians 5:16-18). Without you, I would despair. Thank you for this time when I come with open hands to receive all that you have for me. (John 16:24).

My Joshua 24:15 decision is intact. Today bind Satan from me and my family, Lord, so that we may be a glory to you. Satan is out there waiting, roaming, hunting ways to destroy our witness. Bind him, Lord.

My love, my praise, my thanks belong to you.

Referencing Habakkuk 3

Habakkuk knew God's discipline wasn't going to be pleasant. He accepted God's will, and then he asked for strength and mercy. God still disciplines in love to draw each of us to him--even though the discipline may not be pleasant.

May I be like Habakkuk and rejoice regardless of the circumstances, stay focused on God, and praise him for his faithfulness. May this nation repent, turn to you asking for forgiveness and guidance so the discipline doesn't have to be harsh.

— *Day 23* —

Lord, thank you for today and I praise you for all you have done for me. I want to learn to "acclaim you more as I walk in your presence." (Psalm 89:15). May I fix my eyes on you and run with endurance the race I am in. (Hebrews 12:1-2).

Lord, I know I need you and I thank you for the privilege of dropping your name as I come to the Father in prayer. (1 John 5:12). Teach me to enjoy your presence to the fullest. Remind me of your ever-abiding presence and may I be more intimate with you each day. Strengthen my faith.

Lord, you are wonderfully good to me as I wait for you and seek your face. (Lamentations 3:25.) Your Word (Exodus 23:30) uses phrase "little by little" and "a little at a time." Thank you! Am I stealing your words inappropriately? I do think you are working miracles in answer to my prayers: little by little and a little at a time.

You are faithful. You have a time and a plan that is best for all those who love you. I probably couldn't handle the full blessing if the answers came all at once. And the real blessing—after all— is walking close to you, being in the Light of your presence. Help me trust you for your Perfect Timing. May I follow your directions and surrender completely to you. You do plan good for me and give me your gifts in your Perfect Time.

My Joshua 24:15 decision remains. May I be ready as you decide how you want to use me. I am yours. You are victorious—omnipotent— Lord; bind Satan from me and mine this day. Yes, my love, honor, praise and thanksgiving go to you.

Referencing Lamentations 1

Lord, I pray our nation will turn from our rebellious ways so we will not have to suffer and be humiliated. May we—as a nation—turn to you for strength and guidance; you are our only hope. Immoral living will have consequences. Help us hear your warnings and seek you. May we become *obedient* to your laws; there is freedom. True freedom comes in and from *obedience* to you.

I am saddened by the nation's attitude toward you and your plan for us. May we repent and seek your counsel.

— *Day 24* —

Lord, I don't have any new words of love, praise, honor, and thanksgiving this morning. I just thank you that I can come and be still in your presence and bask in your love. I am constantly aware of my limitations, but there is no limit to your love. May I grasp how wide, long, high, and deep (Ephesians 3:16-19) your love really is; it fills all of space, time, and eternity.

This morning I sense your love and presence, but some day I will see you Face to face. (1 Corinthians 13:12). Until then, this TAG and your Word will be enough. You are still all I need. You are sufficient.

My eternity is guaranteed; I don't doubt that. But, when my trust level drops, I become afraid and then I have to go back to square one. Today, now, I am aware of your presence and place my confidence in the promises I find in your Word. (Psalm 56:3-4). You are faithful. You let me start over and rebuild my trust. Thank you for never changing.

There is such comfort in you Word. David—a man after your heart—felt gloom, doom, apprehension, and despair. (Psalm 6:2-4, 6-8). He knew where to take all that: to you. He acknowledged his weaknesses and walked again. Thank you for your Word.

Today, I reaffirm my commitment to serve you. May Joshua 24:15 be written in my heart. Forgive me when I become afraid and fail you.

Referencing Lamentations 2

Lord, may our nation's worship be true and sincere. May our daily lives reflect your presence in us. May we earnestly seek you, catch a fresh vision of your love and care, and then worship you wholeheartedly.

May we (our nation, cities, churches, families) repent and stop the moral decay that surrounds us. We must repent over the wrongs against you. Sin brings our destruction—not you, Lord. But, all of us are affected by sin's consequences and sin has a way of causing great sorrow. Only when we repent will you rescue us.

— *Day 25* —

Lord, thank you for your presence this morning. I know you know what I am going to say before I say it—and still you come for this private, personal time with me.

You know I don't have a creative writing style and I seem to just repeat myself. You come and you give me strength and refreshment as I allow you to take charge of the day. May I walk purposefully letting you lead me—one step at a time. (Colossians 4:2). Thank you for the abundant blessings you have given me. (1 Thessalonians 5:18).

Lord, you know some of life's events give us an unending grief that we must learn to bear—not necessarily death—sometimes it's the loss of what was hoped for. Thank you because that struggle has been a great teacher drawing me closer to you. It has brought me to you for perfect understanding and comfort. It has given me the assurance that you will make all things right in eternity. (Romans 8:28). I may "weep all night, but joy comes in the morning." (Psalm 30:5).

Lord, I give my private longings and hidden sorrows to you. Only you can make all things beautiful. You are the "Great Recycler"—nothing goes to waste in my life because everything is a part of your master plan. Thank you.

My Joshua 24:15 commitment remains and I ask forgiveness because I have sinned and failed you. (James 5:16). Today may I pick up the "axe head" (2 Kings 6:1-7) and be obedient to you.

I love, honor, and praise you.

Referencing Lamentations 3

In Jeremiah's darkest moments, he was strengthened by the assurance that God had been and would continue to be faithful. You do not change; you are still faithful. Your judgment of sin does not change; neither does your love. (21-23). Your mercy is greater than any sin when we (I) repent.

Help me submit to the "yoke of discipline" (27-33).

Help me:

- be silent as I ponder what you want,

- repent willingly,

- be self-controlled in adversity,

- have confident patience as you lovingly teach me both the long-term and the short-term lessons of my life.

May our nation learn the lesson Jeremiah is teaching about repentance. (Jeremiah 38:6-13). He was put in a well and left to die sinking into the mire, but you rescued him. May this nation that is sinking in sin and mire turn to you in repentance to be brought back to you. I thank you and praise you for your Word.

— *Day 26* —

Lord, thank you for all the blessings you provide here and for the ones your are preparing for me in heaven. (John 14:1-4). Thank you for the security I have as I hold your hand and take the next step. The future belongs to you and that's your secret (Deuteronomy 29:29), but, we are to obey what you have revealed of your plan. Help me trust you completely knowing you are eternal, faithful, and never changing.

Lord, though I am thankful for all the physical blessings you have given me, help me hold onto them only lightly. Help me treat every relationship as a special gift from you—because each one is on loan for a little while. When it is no longer on loan, may I have been a blessing while it lasted and may you be glorified by it.

Truly, Lord, I need you to teach me the "Give no thought for tomorrow" lesson. I am back to square one. I think I've learned it —then think "I've got that and now I am ready for the next lesson." As soon as something changes, I realize I need to relearn lesson one.

You are O, O, O, and O! Omnipotent, Omniscient, Omnipresent and the Omega! You are loving and compassionate and I am yours. You are faithful. You promise to never leave me or forsake me. ***What's my problem? What is there that I can't seem to comprehend and apply to my relationship with you.***

Help me meet my commitment to serve you. You are victorious; bind Satan from me and my house.

I do love you, Lord; I am just weak and pitiful—nothing without you.

Referencing Lamentations 4

I want to learn the lesson you have for me in L-4. I see your warning to our nation of the possibility of losing everything because of sin. Help our nation realize prosperity doesn't mean security; you alone are our security. If we turn our backs on you and worship our wealth, your judgment will be harsh. (Jerusalem was under siege for two years. The enemy now used the walls that had been their protection to seal their doom.)

People had blessings from God and they still turned away. The priests were also evil so there was no spiritual leadership. The people refused to listen to Jeremiah when he said "Rely on God." King Zedekiah listened to false prophets.

Lord, I pray our nation will turn from its evil practices before its too late. May we rely on you.

— Day 27 —

Thank you again this morning for all your unending blessings—
especially this time with you. What would I do without you? Answer:
I would surely fall and fail to get up.

Changes just continue to come in waves—faster and faster. As they
claim more and more of my attention, I lose sight of you. Forgive me,
Lord. Remind me you are always with me and hold me in you powerful
right hand. (Psalm 73:23).

You are omniscient; you know all that's happening here. You are
omnipotent and are in total control. It is your presence that keeps me
standing—and you are omnipresent—always present! One of my most
nagging sins is worrying about tomorrow. You are faithful and will
provide. (1 Corinthians 10:13).

Lord, help me understand what you want me to do—even if it is to be
still and wait for you. (1 Colossians 1:9-12). Give me spiritual wisdom
so that the way I live pleases you and honors you. I want to live in
harmony with others and know you more. Lord, I need your strength
to live joyfully reflecting who you are.

Lord, you held up a mirror for me to see **my** pride and envy this
morning. Now, that I see it, I am asking forgiveness and leaving it
with you. You keep it; don't let me take it back as I have often done
with other sins.

Lord, my relationships with others are woven intricately into my
fellowship with you. I want to have a clear conscience with you and
others so I can be at peace. (Acts 24:16). Give me grace to forgive
others as you have forgiven me.

Transform me so I am presentable to keep my Joshua 24:15 promise to
you. Lord, in your name and power, I am binding Satan from me and
my house. Love, honor, praise, and thanks all go to you.

Referencing Lamentations 5

In a time of grief, we as believers should turn to you to find relief and comfort. Here Jeremiah sees no evidence of healthy interaction among Jerusalem's people. A lack of gratefulness is an indication that God's blessings are taken for granted and a sense of entitlement has developed. There will be bitter suffering when sin catches up with us and God decides he has been patient long enough. The only hope for our nation is repentance! You, Lord, want us to turn to the Father so he can bless us—or you wouldn't have come and he wouldn't have sent you to draw us to you.

Thank you for the eternal life you offer and all the other blessings. Forgive my failings, Lord.

— *Day 28* —

Lord, praise you! Praise you! Praise you! And that still is insufficient! You are worthy of all praise and honor as well as my love and thanksgiving. Nothing I can do is worthy of all you have done for me.

I am not perfect—far from it. I was not a perfect wife or daughter, am not a perfect mother or grandmother, not perfect in any of the roles I have played. The amazing thing is you lived a perfect life for me—died on the cross paying for my sin. And, just because I believe in you, you have wrapped me in a "robe of righteousness" and look on me as I will be when I get to heaven. (Isaiah 61:10). Without that assurance the weight of guilt would be too much to carry.

Today, may I walk along a path with you—one designed for me by you! May we have a continual conversation as we go. I want to bring every detail and circumstance to you, remembering you are as powerful over circumstances as you are over all my sin.

I want to trust you PERFECTLY! You are not on the other side of my circumstances; you are here with me and you are faithful to keep every promise.

This morning I am seeking you and your righteousness first. (Matthew 6:33). Truly all praise, honor, love, and thanksgiving belong to you. May I not seek to glorify myself, but seek ways to glorify you. Keep reminding me that through you I do. I have a hope of heaven.

Imperfect as I am, I am still committed to serving you and I ask you to bind Satan from me and my house.

Love—Honor—Praise—Thanksgiving!

— *Day 29* —

Lord, this TAG is so important to me; thank you for your presence. In this time, as I am focused on you, I can give you my cares and concerns; I am energized. My thoughts aren't as scrambled and I am lighter than I was before I looked to you. Here I am fully aware of your unfailing love. (Psalm 48:9). I also know that I "rest between your shoulders;" you carry me as well as my cares and concerns. (Deuteronomy 33:12). Thank you for your Word—your love letter to me.

Help me surrender—submit—to you and to the Holy Spirit that you left as my comforter and my counselor. I want to trust you completely—enough to surrender. (Philippians 2:13). Help me release my mind and my will to you so you can transform me into the person you desire--to be used according to your good purpose, your pleasing and perfect will. (Romans 12:2).

This morning "you hear my voice and I lay my requests before you and wait in expectation." (Psalm 5:3). I am not alone. Together—with you—I can face a day cheerfully. I cannot face a day dreadfully when I am aware of your presence, because in your presence I find *joy*. You are always present. I just need to always be aware of your presence.

I love you, praise you, and honor you as I thank you.

— *Day 30* —

Lord, out here on my patio this early a.m., I "enter your gates with thanksgiving and your courts with praise. Yes, I give thanks and praise you." (Psalm 100:4). Truly, I am grateful for all my blessings; my greatest blessing is my nearness to you—the joy and peace of your presence. That's my abundant life now and just a glimpse of the abundant life I will have with you in heaven.

Lord, I don't quite get a vivid mental picture of what "worship in spirit and in truth" is, but I want to know. I want to see that in my mind. May the Holy Spirit teach me—show me. (John 4:23-24). I want to be the kind of worshiper you seek.

Show me your way for me this day. Guide me so I can relax and enjoy this day in your presence. May I learn to discipline my thoughts, to trust you and let you transform me into the kind of person you created me to be? I **know** it is only in and through you that everything works for good. (Romans 8:28).

As I take a deep breath and breathe in your love that surrounds me, I want to dive into the depths of absolute trust—trusting you only.

You hear me as I bring my wants and desires to you. I lay my requests at your feet as David did (Psalm 5:2-3) and I wait expectantly.

I love and praise you as I desire to be of service to you.

— *Day 31* —

Lord, I am again in awe of you! "I stand amazed in the presence of Jesus, the Nazarene." I understand what that hymn writer must have felt. The beauty of all your creation, the plan of it all, and the awe that you did it all with just a word. And after that, you tell me you "are doing a new thing." (Isaiah 46:10). I am hoping you are doing a new thing in me.

I am so thankful that you are always with me. That is the basis of my security, and you know I am such a wimp. You died to cover the cost of my sin and then rose from the grave to live forever. (Romans 8:38-39). That is **Victory!** Your Spirit lives in me and I am asking for a filling of your fruit. (Galatians 5:22-23). Continue to grow your fruit in me.

Lord, when I am afraid, I will trust in you. (Psalm 56:3-4). You are trustworthy. You never fail. Again, you are omnipotent, omniscient, omnipresent, and the Omega! What more could I need or ask for! The thought that "in spite of all that you are and all that I am not, you love me" is beyond my comprehension. I don't understand it, but I accept it as fact.

You have blessed me beyond measure and I thank you. I praise you and love you as I leave my cares and concerns with you. I am yours— my cares and concerns also belong to you. Today help me live in a way that glorifies you. Yes, Lord, I want to usable to you.

About the Author

Lee Veasman Rose
Professor Emeritus
College of Business, University of Central Oklahoma
Edmond, OK

After retiring from the University of Central Oklahoma where she was a professor for over 30 years, Lee took her first lesson in basket weaving. It was an instant love affair, and it wasn't long until she taught her first class. She says, "The best thing about basketry is the wonderful people it has brought into my life." I would have never had the opportunity to meet many of the students who later became friends. Basketry gave me a common ground on which to share my love and awe of the Lord and to give encouragement as we wove together.